Wonders Practice Book Grade K Volume 1 Student Edition

create.mheducation.com

Copyright © 2024 by McGraw-Hill Education. All rights reserved.

Printed in the United States of America. Except as permitted under the United States Copyright Act of 1976, no part of this publication may be reproduced or distributed in any form or by any means, or stored in a database or retrieval system, without prior written permission of the publisher.

This McGraw-Hill Create text may include materials submitted to McGraw-Hill for publication by the instructor of this course. The instructor is solely responsible for the editorial content of such materials. Instructors retain copyright of these additional materials.

ISBN-13: 9781309125991

ISBN-10: 1309125996

Contents

Wonders Practice Book Grade K Volume 1 Student Edition   1
Credits   277

Contents

START SMART

Week 1

Concepts of Print 3
Phonological Awareness: Sentence
Segmentation 4
Phonological Awareness: Nursery Rhyme 5
Letter Identification 6–10
Category Words: Names 11
High-Frequency Words: *I* 12
Take-Home Story 13–14

Week 2

Concepts of Print 15
Phonological Awareness: Sentence
Segmentation 16
Phonological Awareness: Nursery Rhyme 17
Letter Identification 18–22
Category Words: Numbers 23
High-Frequency Words: *can* 24
Take-Home Story 25–26

Week 3

Concepts of Print 27
Phonological Awareness:
Recognize Syllables 28
Phonological Awareness: Nursery Rhyme 29
Letter Identification 30–34
Category Words: Days of the Week 35
High-Frequency Words: *I, can* 36
Take-Home Story 37–38

Grade K • Start Smart   iii

Contents

UNIT 1
Take a New Step

Week 1
- Phonological Awareness: Sentence Segmentation 39
- Phonemic Awareness: Phoneme Isolation 40
- Phoneme Blending 41
- Phonics: Initial/final /m/*m* 42
- Handwriting 43
- High-Frequency Words: *the* 44
- Category Words: Feeling Words 45
- Grammar: Nouns/Edit/Proofread 46–48
- Take-Home Story 49–50

Week 2
- Phonological Awareness: Recognize Rhyme 51
- Phonemic Awareness: Phoneme Isolation 52
- Phoneme Blending 53
- Phonics: Initial/medial /a/*a* 54
- Handwriting 55
- High-Frequency Words: *we, can* 56
- Category Words: *Family Words* 57
- Grammar: Nouns/Edit/Proofread 58–60
- Take-Home Story 61–62

Week 3
- Phonological Awareness: Onset/Rime Blending 63
- Phonemic Awareness: Phoneme Isolation 64
- Phoneme Blending 65
- Phonics: Initial /s/*s* 66
- Handwriting 67
- High-Frequency Words: *see, the* 68
- Category Words: Sensory Words 69
- Grammar: Nouns/Edit/Proofread 70–72
- Take-Home Story 73–74

UNIT 2
Let's Explore

Week 1
- Phonological Awareness: Alliteration 75
- Phonemic Awareness: Phoneme Isolation 76
- Phoneme Blending 77
- Phonics: Initial/final /p/*p* 78
- Phonics/Spelling 79
- Phonics: Letter/Sound Match 80
- Handwriting 81
- High-Frequency Words: *a, see* 82
- Category Words: Colors 83
- Grammar: Verbs/Edit/Proofread 84–86
- Take-Home Story 87–88

Week 2
- Phonological Awareness: Onset/Rime Blending 89
- Phonemic Awareness: Phoneme Isolation 90
- Phoneme Blending 91
- Phonics: Initial/final /t/*t* 92
- Phonics/Spelling 93
- Phonics: Letter/Sound Match 94
- Handwriting 95
- High-Frequency Words: *like, a* 96
- Category Words: Colors 97
- Grammar: Verbs/Edit/Proofread 98–100
- Take-Home Story 101–102

Week 3
- Phonological Awareness: Count and Pronounce Syllables 103
- Phonics: Letter Review 104–105
- Phonics/Spelling 106
- High-Frequency Words Review 107
- Category Words: Textures 108
- Category Words Review 109
- Grammar: Verbs/Edit/Proofread 110–112
- Take-Home Story 113–114

UNIT 3
Going Places

Week 1
Phonological Awareness: Recognize Rhyme ...115
Phonemic Awareness: Phoneme Isolation 116
Phoneme Blending 117
Phonics: Initial/medial /i/i.................................. 118
Phonics/Spelling 119
Phonics: Letter/Sound Match 120
Handwriting 121
High-Frequency Words: to, like........................... 122
Category Words: Action Words 123
Grammar: Adjectives/Edit/Proofread........ 124–126
Take-Home Story 127–128

Week 2
Phonological Awareness:
Onset and Rime Blending..................................129
Phonemic Awareness: Phoneme Isolation 130
Phoneme Blending 131
Phonics: Initial/final /n/n.................................. 132
Phonics/Spelling 133
Phonics: Letter/Sound Match 134
Handwriting 135
High-Frequency Words: and, to........................ 136
Category Words: Sound Words........................ 137
Grammar: Sentences/Edit/Proofread 138–140
Take-Home Story 141–142

Week 3
Phonological Awareness:
Count and Pronounce Syllables............................143
Phonemic Awareness: Phoneme Isolation 144
Phoneme Identity 145
Phonics: Initial /k/c 146
Phonics/Spelling 147
Phonics: Letter/Sound Match 148
Handwriting 149
High-Frequency Words: go, and......................... 150
Category Words: Sequence Words..................... 151
Grammar: Sentences/Edit/Proofread 152–153
Take-Home Story 155–156

UNIT 4
Around the Neighborhood

Week 1
Phonological Awareness:
Onset/Rime Segmentation.................................157
Phonemic Awareness:
Phoneme Isolation.. 158
Phoneme Blending 159
Phonics: Initial/medial /o/o............................... 160
Phonics/Spelling 161
Phonics: Letter/Sound Match 162
Handwriting 163
High-Frequency Words: you, go........................ 164
Category Words: Job Words...............................165
Grammar: Adjectives/Edit/Proofread........ 166–168
Take-Home Story 169–170

Week 2
Phonological Awareness:
Sentence Segmentation......................................171
Phonemic Awareness: Phoneme Isolation 172
Phoneme Segmentation 173
Phonics: Initial/final /d/d..................................174
Phonics/Spelling 175
Phonics: Letter/Sound Match 176
Handwriting 177
High-Frequency Words: do, you........................ 178
Category Words: Kinds of Foods.........................179
Grammar: Adjectives/Edit/Proofread....... 180–182
Take-Home Story 183–184

Week 3
Phonological Awareness:
Recognize Rhyme 185
Phonics Review 186
Phonics: Blends sn, sp, st................................. 187
Phonics/Spelling 188
High-Frequency Words Review............................ 189
Category Words: Position Words....................... 190
Category Words Review 191
Grammar: Adjectives/Edit/Proofread........192–194
Take-Home Story 195–196

Grade K • Unit 3 • Unit 4

UNIT 5
Wonders of Nature

Week 1

Phonological Awareness:
Count and Blend Syllables 197
Phonemic Awareness: Phoneme Isolation 198
Phoneme Categorization 199
Phonics Initial: /h/h 200
Phonics/Spelling 201
Phonics: Letter/Sound Match 202
Handwriting 203
High-Frequency Words: *my, you* 204
Category Words: Size Words 205
Grammar: Pronouns/Edit/Proofread 206–208
Take-Home Story 209–210

Week 2

Phonological Awareness:
Onset/Rime Blending 211
Phonemic Awareness: Phoneme Isolation 212
Phoneme Segmentation 213
Phonics: Initial/medial /e/e 214
Phonics/Spelling 215
Phonics: Letter/Sound Match 216
Handwriting 217
High-Frequency Words: *are, my* 218
Category Words: Tree Parts 219
Grammar: Pronouns/Edit/Proofread 220–222
Take-Home Story 223–224

Week 3

Phonological Awareness:
Recognize Rhyme 225
Phonemic Awareness:
Phoneme Isolation 226–227
Phoneme Addition 228
Phonics: Initial/final /f/f, /r/r 229–230
Phonics/Spelling 231
Phonics: Minimal Contrasts 232
Handwriting 233
High-Frequency Words: *with, he, are* 234
Category Words: Foods 235
Grammar: Pronouns/Edit/Proofread 236–238
Take-Home Story 239–240

UNIT 6
Weather for All Seasons

Week 1

Phonological Awareness:
Onset/Rime Segmentation 241
Phonemic Awareness:
Phoneme Isolation 242–243
Phoneme Blending 244
Phonics: Initial/final /b/b, Initial /l/l 245–246
Phonics/Spelling 247
Phonics: Minimal Contrasts 248
Handwriting 249
High-Frequency Words: *is, little, my* 250
Category Words: Seasons 251
Grammar: Plural Nouns/Edit/
Proofread 252–254
Take-Home Story 255–256

Week 2

Phonological Awareness: Rhyme 257
Phonemic Awareness:
Phoneme Isolation 258–259
Phoneme Segmentation 260
Phonics: Initial /k/k, Final /k/ck 261–262
Phonics/Spelling 263
Phonics: Minimal Contrasts 264
Handwriting 265
High-Frequency Words: *she, was, little* 266
Category Words: Weather Words 267
Grammar: Proper Nouns/Edit/
Proofread 268–270
Take-Home Story 271–272

Week 3

Phonological Awareness: Alliteration 273
Phonics Review 274–276
Phonics: Blends *bl, cl, fl, sl* 277
Phonics/Spelling 278
High-Frequency Words Review: 279
Category Words: Question Words 280
Category Words Review 281
Grammar: Proper Nouns/Edit/
Proofread 282–284
Take-Home Story 285–286

UNIT 7
The Animal Kingdom

Week 1

Phonological Awareness:
Onset/Rime Blending 287
Phonemic Awareness: Phoneme Isolation 288
Phoneme Deletion 289
Phonics: Initial/medial /u/*u* 290
Phonics/Spelling 291
Phonics: Letter/Sound Match 292
Handwriting 293
High-Frequency Words: *for, have, with* 294
Category Words: Animal Parts 295
Grammar: Verbs/Edit/Proofread 296-298
Take-Home Story 299-300

Week 2

Phonological Awareness:
Recognize and Generate Rhyme 301
Phonemic Awareness:
Phoneme Isolation 302-303
Phoneme Substitution 304
Phonics: Initial/final /g/*g*, Initial /w/*w* 305-306
Phonics/Spelling 307
Phonics: Minimal Contrasts 308
Handwriting 309
High-Frequency Words: *of, they, for* 310
Category Words: Pets 311
Grammar: Verbs/Edit/Proofread 312-314
Take-Home Story 315-316

Week 3

Phonological Awareness:
Onset/Rime Segmentation 317
Phonemic Awareness:
Phoneme Isolation 318-319
Phoneme Substitution 320
Phonics: Final /ks/*x*, Initial /v/*v* 321-322
Phonics/Spelling 323
Phonics: Minimal Contrasts 324
Handwriting 325
High-Frequency Words: *said, want, have* 326
Category Words: Animal Homes 327
Grammar: Verbs/Edit/Proofread 328-330
Take-Home Story 331-332

UNIT 8
From Here to There

Week 1

Phonological Awareness: Syllable Addition ... 333
Phonemic Awareness:
Phoneme Isolation 334-335
Phoneme Segmentation 336
Phonics: Initial /j/*j*, /kw/*qu* 337-338
Phonics/Spelling 339
Phonics: Minimal Contrasts 340
Handwriting 341
High-Frequency Words; *here, me, want* 342
Category Words: Vehicles 343
Grammar: Sentences/Edit/Proofread 344-346
Take-Home Story 347-348

Week 2

Phonological Awareness:
Generate Rhyme 349
Phonemic Awareness:
Phoneme Isolation 350-351
Phoneme Substitution 352
Phonics: Initial /y/*y*, /z/*z* 353-354
Phonics/Spelling 355
Phonics: Minimal Contrasts 356
Handwriting 357
High-Frequency Words: *this, what, me* 358
Category Words: Location Words 359
Grammar: Sentences/Edit/Proofread 360-362
Take-Home Story 363-364

Week 3

Phonological Awareness: Syllable Deletion ... 365
Phonics Review 366-368
Phonics: Blends: *br, cr, dr, gr, tr* 369
Phonics/Spelling 370
High-Frequency Words Review 371
Category Words: Opposites 372
Category Words Review 373
Grammar: Sentences/Edit/Proofread 374-376
Take-Home Story 377-378

UNIT 9
How Things Change

Week 1

Phonological Awareness:
Syllable Segmentation 379
Phonemic Awareness: Phoneme Identity 380
Phoneme Blending 381
Phonics: Long a: *a_e* 382
Phonics/Spelling 383
Phonics: Minimal Contrasts 384
Handwriting 385
High-Frequency Words: *help, too, here* 386
Category Words: Household Furniture 387
Grammar: Adjectives/Edit/Proofread 388–390
Take-Home Story 391–392

Week 2

Phonological Awareness: Generate Rhyme ... 393
Phonemic Awareness: Phoneme Identity 394
Phoneme Deletion 395
Phonics: Long i: *i_e* 396
Phonics/Spelling 397
Phonics: Minimal Contrasts 398
Handwriting 399
High-Frequency Words: *has, play, too* 400
Category Words: Farm Animals 401
Grammar: Adjectives/Edit/Proofread 402–404
Take-Home Story 405–406

Week 3

Phonological Awareness:
Count and Blend Syllables 407
Phonemic Awareness: Phoneme Identity 408
Phoneme Substitution 409
Phonics: Long o: *o_e* 410
Phonics/Spelling 411
Phonics: Minimal Contrasts 412
Handwriting 413
High-Frequency Words: *where, look, play* ... 414
Category Words: Foods Made from Grain 415
Grammar: Adjectives/Edit/Proofread 416–418
Take-Home Story 419–420

UNIT 10
Thinking Outside the Box

Week 1

Phonological Awareness:
Segmenting Syllables 421
Phonemic Awareness:
Phoneme Identity 422
Phoneme Substitution 423
Phonics: Long u: *u_e* 424
Phonics/Spelling 425
Phonics: Minimal Contrasts 426
Handwriting 427
High-Frequency Words: *good, who, where* .. 428
Category Words: Direction Words 429
Grammar: Pronouns/Edit/Proofread 430–432
Take-Home Story 433–434

Week 2

Phonological Awareness:
Syllable Substitution 435
Phonemic Awareness:
Phoneme Identity 436
Phoneme Substitution 437
Phonics: Long e: *e, ee, e_e* 438
Phonics/Spelling 439
Phonics: Minimal Contrasts 440
Handwriting 441
High-Frequency Words: *come, does, who* 442
Category Words: Opposites 443
Grammar: Pronouns/Edit/Proofread 444–446
Take-Home Story 447–448

Week 3

Phonological Awareness: Alliteration 449
Phonics Review 450–452
Phonics: Final Blends: *st, nd, nk* 453
Phonics/Spelling 454
High-Frequency Words Review 455
Category Words: Names of Baby Animals 456
Category Words Review 457
Grammar: Pronouns/Edit/Proofread 458–460
Take-Home Story 461–462

Backmatter 463–514
My Strategies and Tools 515

Name _____

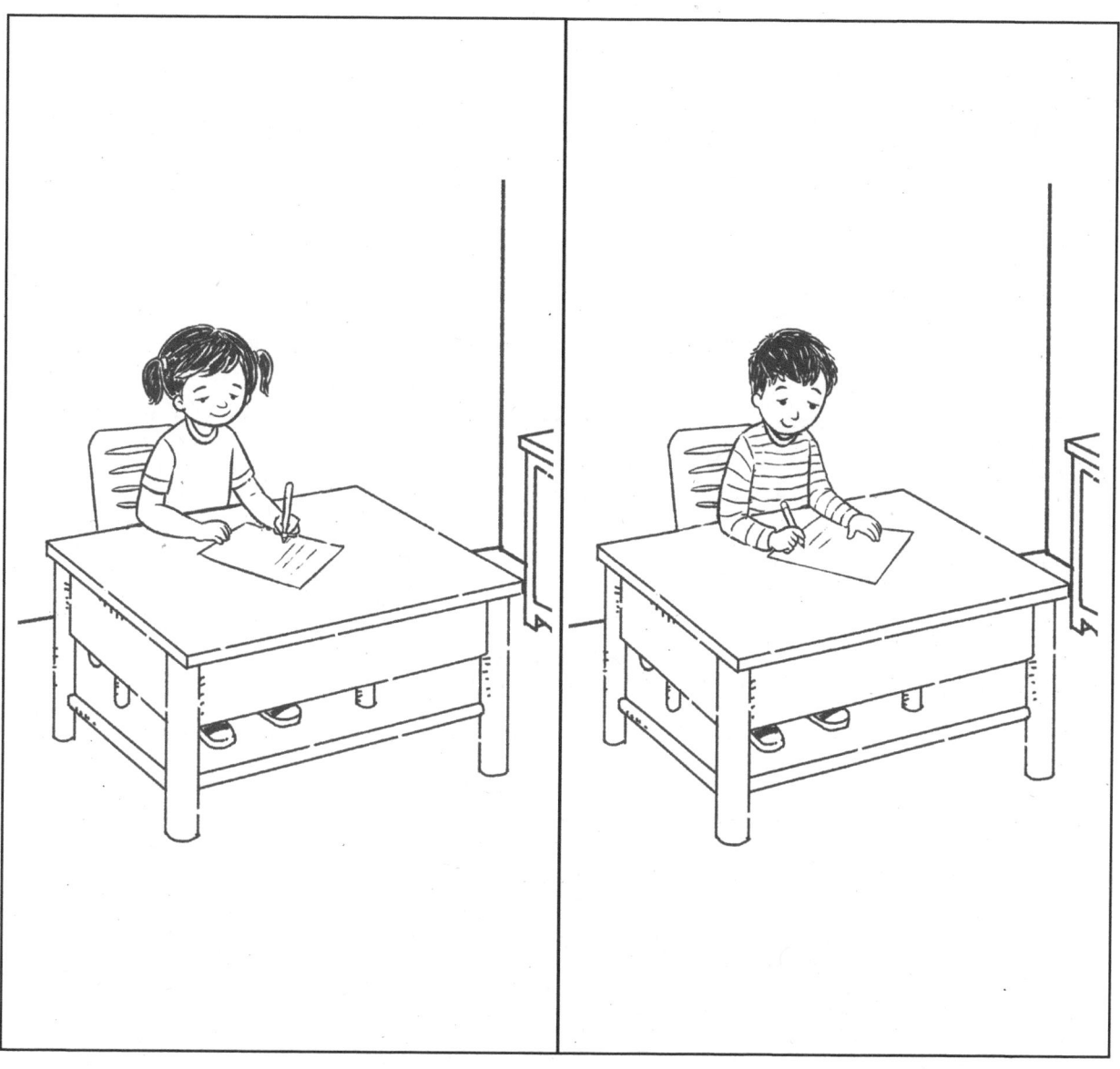

Handwriting
Model for children the correct way to sit up, hold a pencil, and have the correct paper placement. Say: *The picture on the left shows the way a left-handed person writes. The picture on the right shows the way a right-handed person writes.* Then tell children to sit up straight with their feet on the floor. Have them practice sitting up straight, holding a pencil, and slanting their paper.

Grade K 1

Name _____

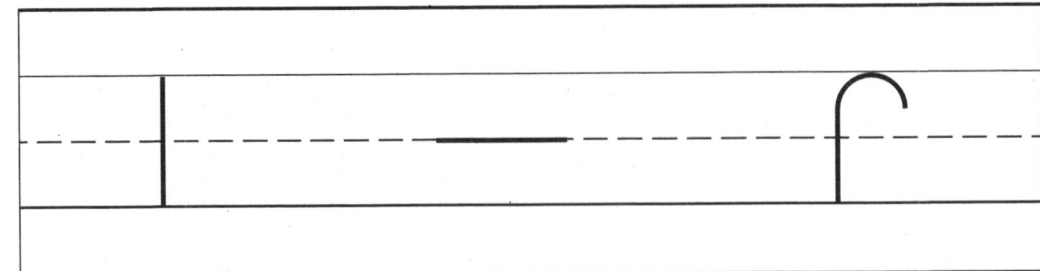

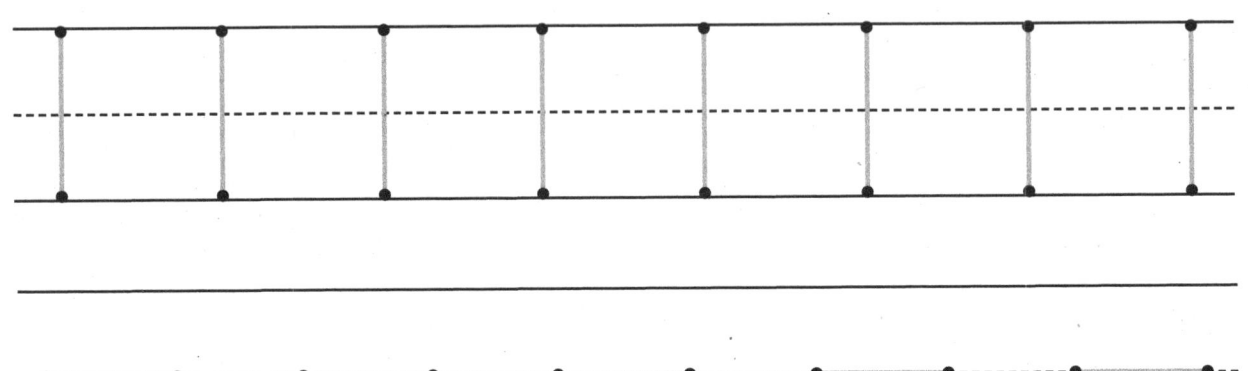

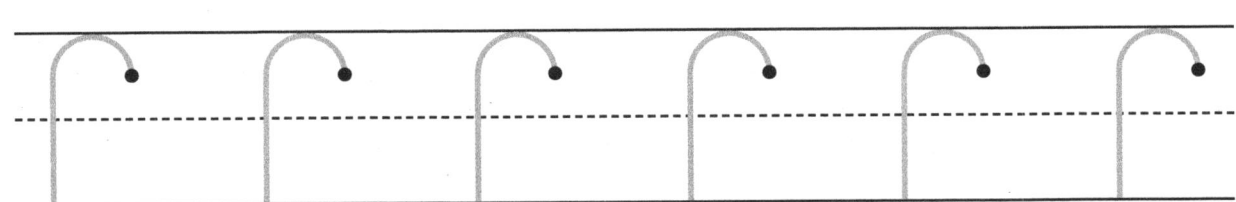

Letter Formation
Point to the first letter form at the top of the page. Explain to children that some letters are formed using a straight line that goes up and down. Point to the second letter form and tell children that other letters are formed with straight lines that go from left to right. Point to the third letter form and explain that still other letters are formed using a curved line and a straight line. Tell children to then trace the letter forms in each row.

Name _____

Concepts of Print
Show children the front cover, the back cover, and the title page of *Animals in the Park*. Explain what each one shows. Model these concepts of print. Then have children do the following:
🍎 Circle the picture that shows the back cover.
★ Circle the picture that shows the front cover.
🌲 Circle the picture that shows the title page.

Grade K • Start Smart • Week 1 **3**

Name _____

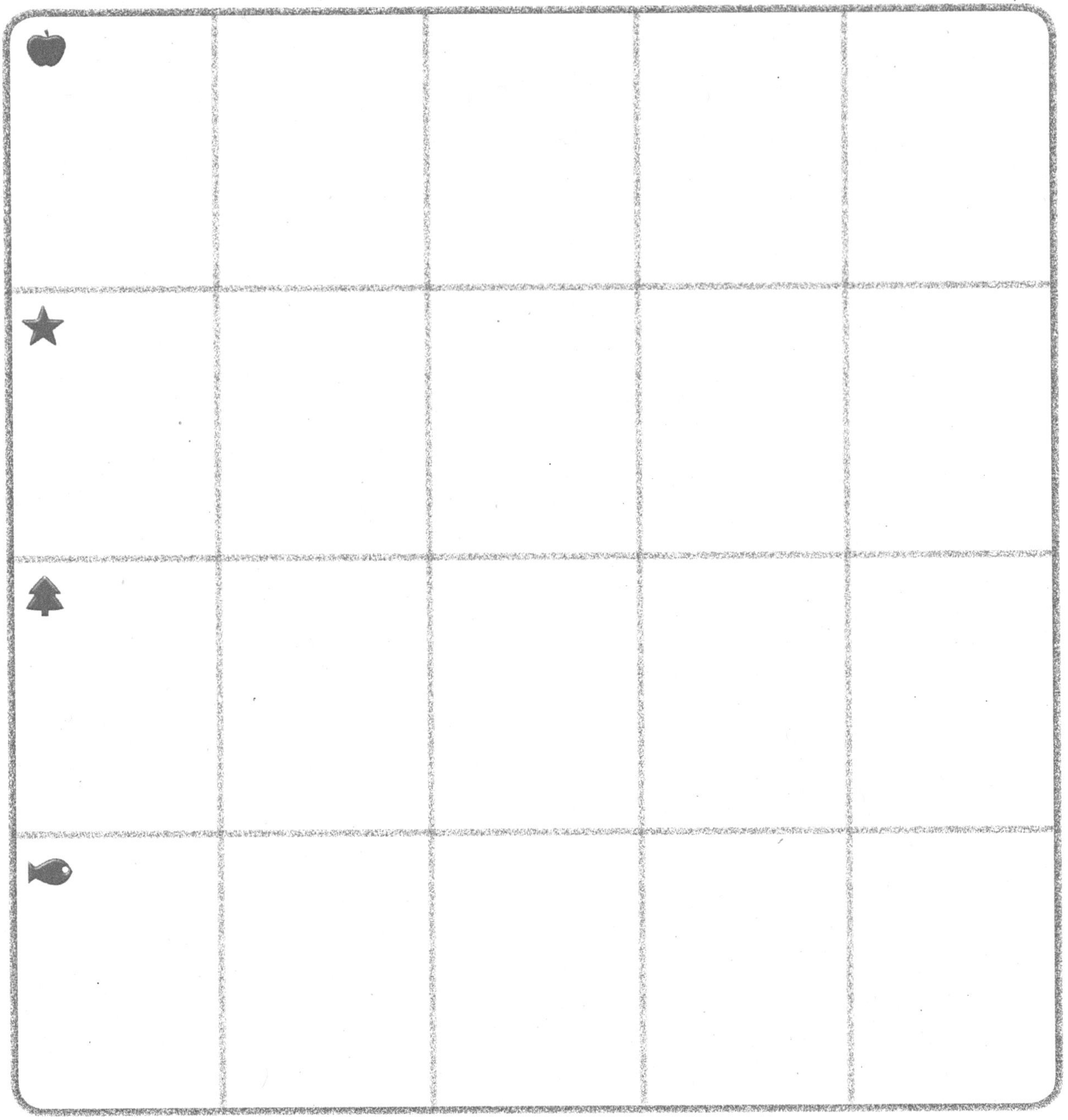

Phonological Awareness: Sentence Segmentation
Explain to children that sentences are made up of words. Say: *I like to learn.* Tell children that there are four words in the sentence. Hold up a finger for each word in the sentence. Tell children you will color in four boxes to show that there are four words in the sentence. Then tell children to color in a box for each word that they hear in the following sentences: ★ *It is sunny out.* 🌲 *Please turn to page four.* 🐟 *I can.* Then have children identify the words in each of the sentences.

Name _____

Phonological Awareness: Nursery Rhyme
Explain to children that a nursery rhyme is a short rhyme that tells a story. It also has a beat or rhythm. Tell children that you will read the nursery rhyme "Humpty Dumpty" aloud. Encourage them to listen as you clap to the beat. Say: *The beat that you hear is the rhythm.* Repeat the rhyme again, this time asking children to clap to the beat. Tell children to also listen for rhyming words, or words that end the same way as in *net* and *pet*. Draw a picture of something that rhymes with the picture of the wall in the first row and discuss with children. Then have them draw something that rhymes with the other picture names.

Grade K • Start Smart • Week 1

Name _____

Aa Bb Cc Dd Ee Ff Gg Hh Ii Jj Kk Ll Mm
Nn Oo Pp Qq Rr Ss Tt Uu Vv Ww Xx Yy Zz

Letter Recognition: *Aa*
Point to and say the uppercase and lowercase forms of the letter *Aa*. Tell children that the uppercase *A* is used if it's the first word in a sentence or the first letter in a person's name, such as *Amy*. Tell children to draw a line from each uppercase letter *A* to each lowercase *a* on the page.

6 Grade K • Start Smart • Week 1

Name _____

Aa Bb Cc Dd Ee Ff Gg Hh Ii Jj Kk Ll Mm
Nn Oo Pp Qq Rr Ss Tt Uu Vv Ww Xx Yy Zz

Letter Recognition: *Bb*
Point to and say the uppercase and lowercase forms of the letter *Bb*. Tell children that the uppercase *B* is used if it's the first word in a sentence or the first letter in a person's name, such as *Bonnie*. Tell children to draw a line from each uppercase letter *B* to each lowercase *b* on the page.

Name _____

Aa Bb Cc Dd Ee Ff Gg Hh Ii Jj Kk Ll Mm
Nn Oo Pp Qq Rr Ss Tt Uu Vv Ww Xx Yy Zz

Letter Recognition: Cc, Dd
Point to and say the uppercase and lowercase forms of the letter *Cc*. Tell children that the uppercase *C* is used if it's the first word in a sentence or the first letter in a person's name, such as *Carol*. Tell children to draw a line from each uppercase *C* to each lowercase *c* on the page. Repeat with the uppercase and lowercase forms of the letter *Dd* and the name *Dan*.

Name _____

Aa Bb Cc Dd Ee Ff Gg Hh Ii Jj Kk Ll Mm
Nn Oo Pp Qq Rr Ss Tt Uu Vv Ww Xx Yy Zz

Letter Recognition: *Ee, Ff*
Point to and say the uppercase and lowercase forms of the letter *Ee*. Tell children that the uppercase *E* is used if it's the first word in a sentence or the first letter in a person's name, such as *Ed*. Tell children to draw a line from each uppercase letter *E* to each lowercase *e*. Repeat with the uppercase and lowercase forms of the letter *Ff* and the name *Finn*.

Name _____

Aa Bb Cc Dd Ee Ff Gg Hh Ii Jj Kk Ll Mm
Nn Oo Pp Qq Rr Ss Tt Uu Vv Ww Xx Yy Zz

Letter Recognition: *Gg, Hh*
Point to and say the uppercase and lowercase forms of the letter *Gg*. Tell children that the uppercase *G* is used if it's the first word in a sentence or the first letter in a person's name, such as *Gabe*. Tell children to draw a line from each uppercase letter *G* to each lowercase letter *g*. Repeat with the uppercase and lowercase forms of the letter *Hh* and the name *Hannah*.

10 Grade K • Start Smart • Week 1

Name _____

Category Words: Names
Explain to children that people have names to identify them, such as *Amy* and *Dave*. Tell children that some of the pictures on this page show children with names. Point to and name the pictures in each row. Have children circle the pictures that show names. Then have partners use the names in sentences.

Grade K • Start Smart • Week 1   11

 Name _____

High-Frequency Words: *I*

Model the Read/Spell/Write routine using the word *I*. Have children repeat the routine. Point to and say the names of the picture in each row. Then have children write the word *I* on the line to complete each sentence. Then say the word *I* for children to spell. Then have pairs of children read each sentence to a partner. Encourage children to point to the word *I* as they read.

12 Grade K • Start Smart • Week 1

Name _____

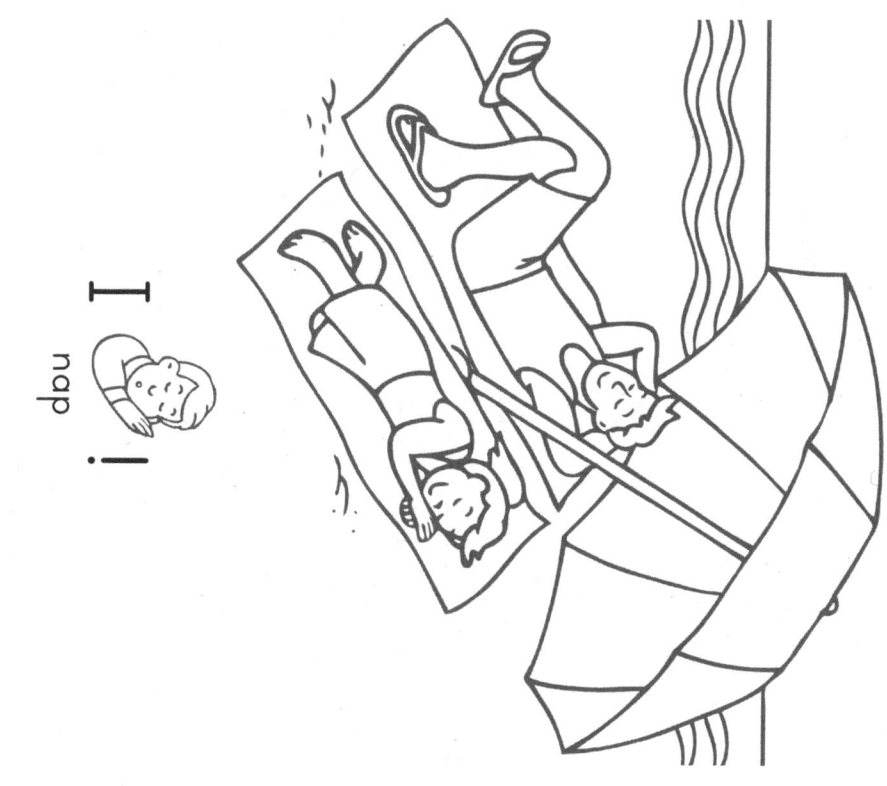

I nap.

Review High-Frequency Words
Have children set a purpose for reading, such as finding out what the boy and girl can do. Explain that words in a sentence are separated by spaces. Model pointing to the space between words. Then ask children to point to the space between the word *I* and the rebus of the boy hopping on page 1.

TEKS: K.(5)(A), K.(2)(B)(iv), K.(2)(D)(iii)

I hop.

Connect to Community
Encourage children to read the story to a family member or a friend.

4 Grade K · Start Smart · Week 1

I dig.

I throw.

Name _____

Concepts of Print
Show children the front cover, the back cover, and the title page of *The Big Book of Rhymes*. Explain what each one shows. Model these concepts of print. Then have children do the following:
🍎 Circle the picture that shows the front cover.
★ Circle the picture that shows the title page.
🌲 Circle the picture that shows the back cover.

Grade K • Start Smart • Week 2 15

Name _____

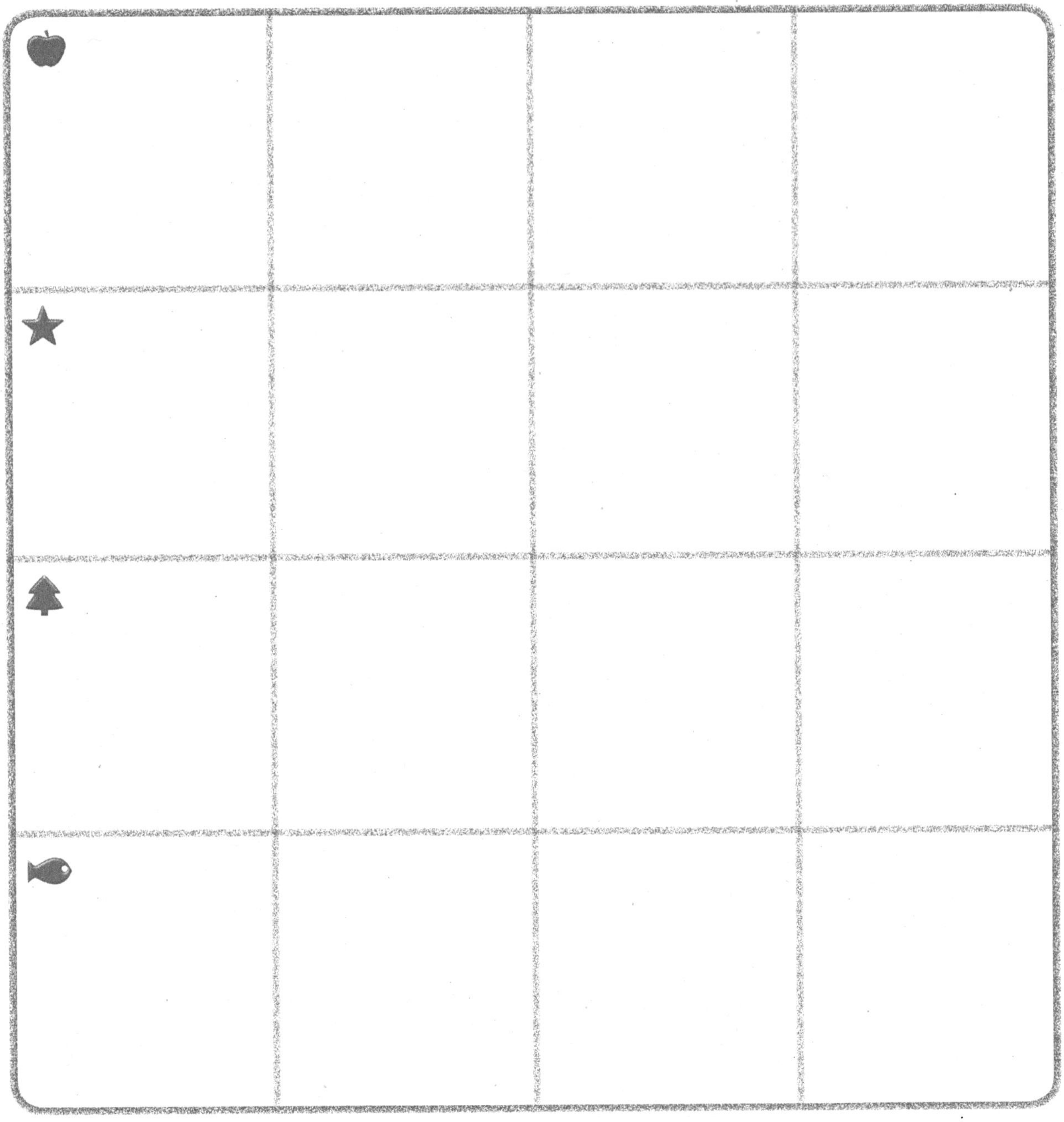

Phonological Awareness: Sentence Segmentation
Explain to children that sentences are made up of words. Say: *We raise our hands.* Tell children that there are four words in the sentence. Hold up a finger for each word in the sentence. Tell children you will color in four boxes to show that there are four words in the sentence. Then tell children to color in a box for each word that they hear in the following sentences: ★ *I ate a sandwich.* ▲ *You can go.* 🐟 *Can you help?* Then have children identify the individual words in each sentence.

Name _____

🍎 (fish picture)	
⭐ 10	
🌲 3	
🐟 1	

Phonological Awareness: Nursery Rhyme
Explain to children that a nursery rhyme is a short rhyme that tells a story. Point out that a nursery rhyme has a beat or rhythm. Tell children that you will read the nursery rhyme "1, 2, 3, 4, 5" aloud. Clap to the beat as you read the rhyme. Repeat the rhyme, this time asking children to clap to the beat. Encourage children to listen for rhyming words, or words that end the same way as in *mat* and *pat*. Tell children to draw a picture of something that rhymes with the name of the picture in each row.

Name _____

Aa Bb Cc Dd Ee Ff Gg Hh Ii Jj Kk Ll Mm
Nn Oo Pp Qq Rr Ss Tt Uu Vv Ww Xx Yy Zz

Letter Recognition: *Ii, Jj*
Point to and say the uppercase and lowercase forms of the letter *Ii*. Tell children that the uppercase letter *I* is used if it's the first word in a sentence or the first letter in a person's name, such as *Ingrid*. Tell children to draw a line from each uppercase letter *I* to each lowercase *i*. Repeat with the uppercase and lowercase forms of the letter *Jj* and the name *Jack*.

Name _____

Aa Bb Cc Dd Ee Ff Gg Hh Ii Jj Kk Ll Mm
Nn Oo Pp Qq Rr Ss Tt Uu Vv Ww Xx Yy Zz

Letter Recognition: *Kk, Ll*
Point to and say the uppercase and lowercase forms of the letter *Kk*. Tell children that the uppercase letter *K* is used if it's the first word in a sentence or the first letter in a person's name, such as *Ken*. Tell children to draw a line from each uppercase letter *K* to each lowercase *k*. Repeat with the uppercase and lowercase forms of the letter *Ll* and the name *Lee*.

Grade K • Start Smart • Week 2   19

Name _____

Aa Bb Cc Dd Ee Ff Gg Hh Ii Jj Kk Ll Mm
Nn Oo Pp Qq Rr Ss Tt Uu Vv Ww Xx Yy Zz

Letter Recognition: Mm, Nn
Point to and say the uppercase and lowercase forms of the letter *Mm*. Tell children that the uppercase letter *M* is used if it's the first word in a sentence or the first letter in a person's name, such as *Meg*. Tell children to draw a line from each uppercase letter *M* to each lowercase *m*. Repeat with the uppercase and lowercase forms of the letter *Nn* and the name *Nan*.

Name _____

Aa Bb Cc Dd Ee Ff Gg Hh Ii Jj Kk Ll Mm
Nn Oo Pp Qq Rr Ss Tt Uu Vv Ww Xx Yy Zz

Letter Recognition: *Oo, Pp*
Point to and say the uppercase and lowercase forms of the letter *Oo*. Tell children that the uppercase letter *O* is used if it's the first word in a sentence or the first letter in a person's name, such as *Olivia*. Tell children to draw a line from each uppercase letter *O* to each lowercase *o*. Repeat with the uppercase and lowercase forms of the letter *Pp* and the name *Pam*.

Grade K • Start Smart • Week 2 **21**

Name _____

Aa Bb Cc Dd Ee Ff Gg Hh Ii Jj Kk Ll Mm
Nn Oo Pp Qq Rr Ss Tt Uu Vv Ww Xx Yy Zz

Letter Recognition: *Qq, Rr*
Point to and say the uppercase and lowercase forms of the letter *Qq*. Tell children that the uppercase letter *Q* is used if it's the first word in a sentence or the first letter in a person's name, such as *Quinn*. Tell children to draw a line from each uppercase letter *Q* to each lowercase *q*. Repeat with the uppercase and lowercase forms of the letter *Rr* and the name *Robert*.

Name _____

🍎

5   D   10

⭐

2   4   a

🌲

L   3   7

Category Words: Numbers
Explain to children that they will be learning numbers in addition to letters. Say: *A number tells how many there are of something.* Say: *Ten is a number. There are 10 children in the library.* Tell children that some of the pictures on this page show numbers. Point to and name the numbers and letters in each row. Have children circle the pictures that show numbers.

 Name _____

 I _____

 I _____

 I _____

 I _____

High-Frequency Words: *can*
Model the Read/Spell/Write routine using the word *can*. Have children repeat the routine. Point to and say the names of the picture in each row. Then have children write the word *can* on the line to complete each sentence. Say the words *I* and *can* for children to spell. Encourage pairs of children to tell each other what they can do.

Name _____

I Can
hug
!

Connect to Community
Encourage children to read the story to a family member or a friend.

4

Grade K • Start Smart • Week 2

I can hug!

I can 👀 see !

Review High-Frequency Words
Have children set a purpose for reading, such as finding out what the girl can do. Explain that words in a sentence are separated by spaces. Model pointing to the space between the words I and can on page 1. Then tell children to point to the space between the words I and can on page 4.

TEKS: K.(5)(A), K.(2)(D)(iii)

1

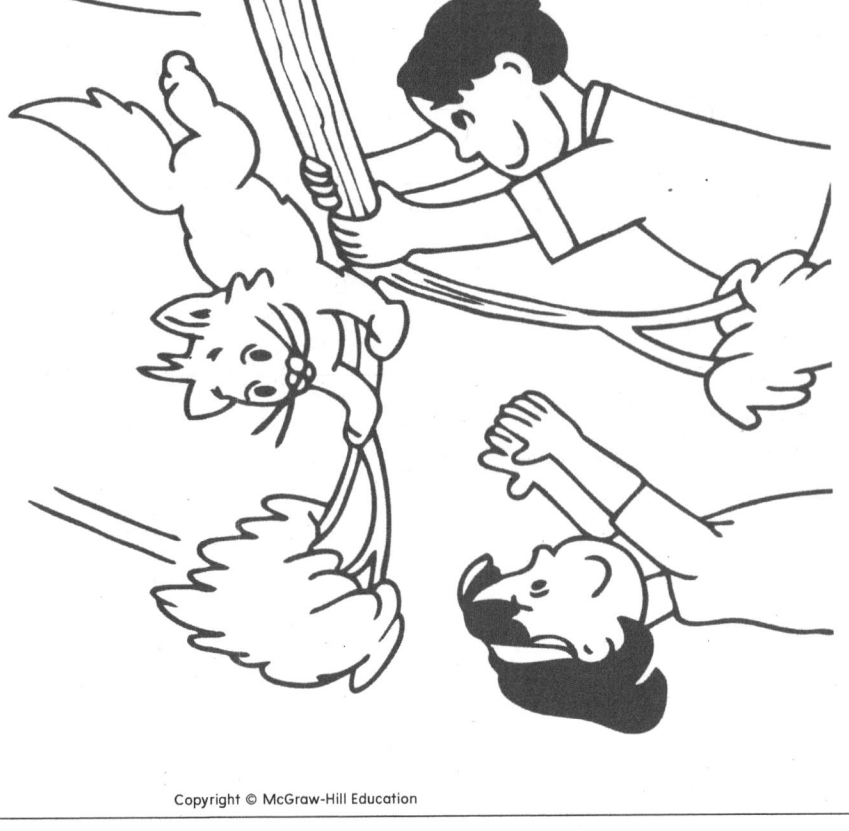

I can  catch.

I can  yell.

Name _____

Concepts of Print
Show children the front cover, the back cover, and the title page of *Ana Goes to Washington, D.C.* Explain what each one shows. Model these concepts of print. Then have children do the following:
🍎 Circle the picture that shows the front cover.
★ Circle the picture that shows the title page.
🌲 Circle the picture that shows the back cover.

 Name _____

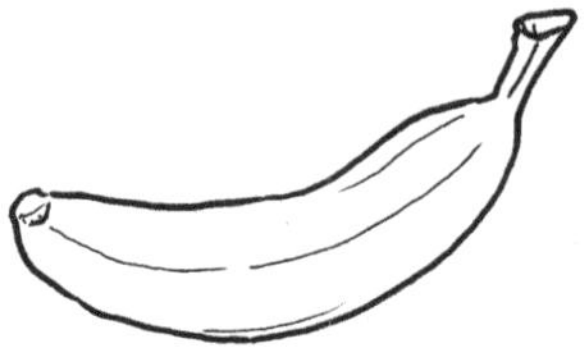

Phonological Awareness: Recognize Syllables
Point to the apple and say its name. Model clapping for each syllable or part in the word. Point out that there are two parts or syllables in *apple*. Tell children that you will write the number 2 in the box because *apple* has two parts or syllables. Point to and name the picture in each row. Tell children to write a number in the box next to the picture to show how many parts or syllables they hear. Then have children identify the parts or syllables in each word.

28 Grade K • Start Smart • Week 3

Name _____

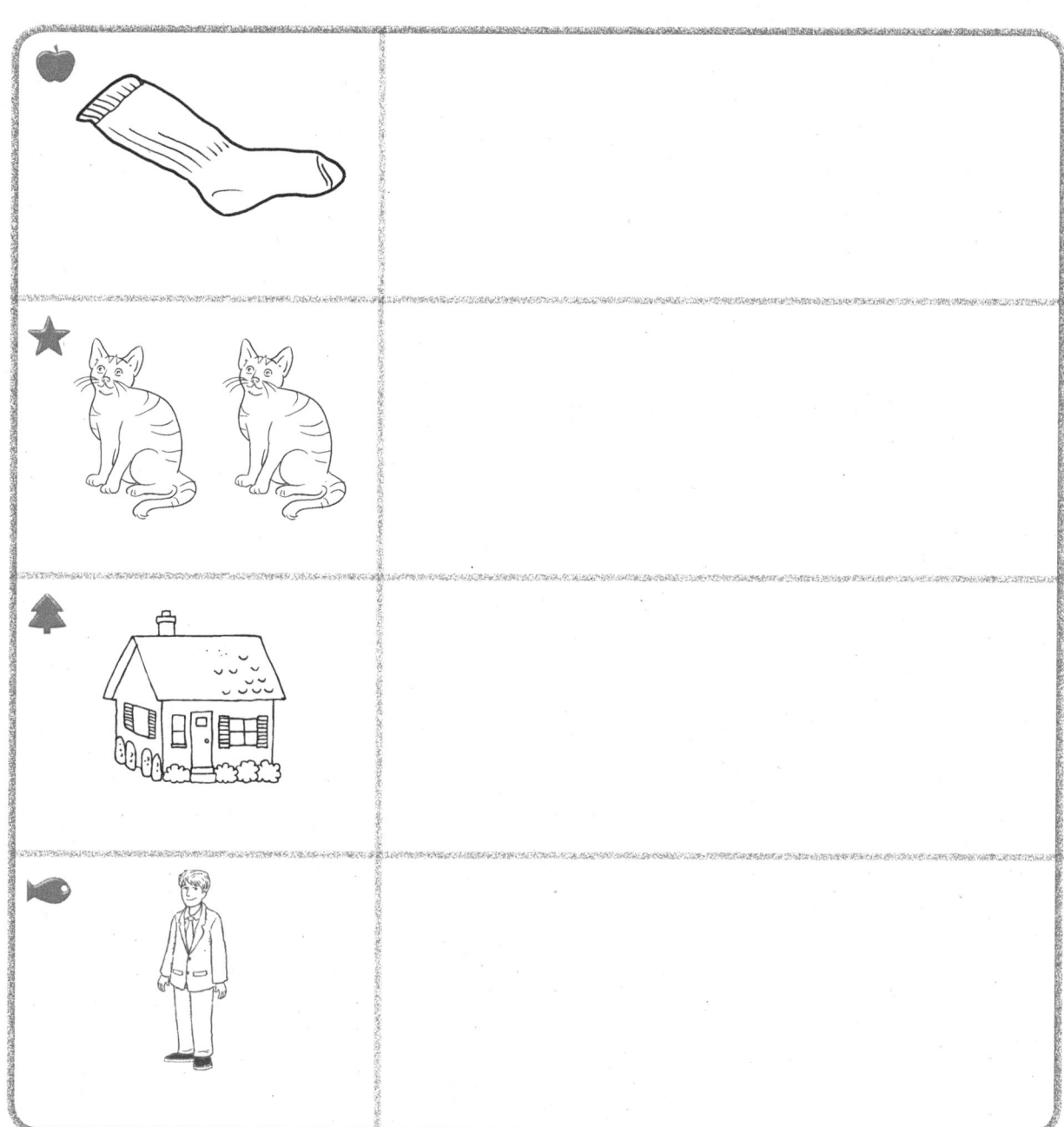

Phonological Awareness: Nursery Rhyme
Explain to children that a nursery rhyme is a short rhyme that tells a story. Tell children that you will read the nursery rhyme "As I Was Going to St. Ives" aloud. Encourage them to listen for rhyming words, or words that end the same way as in *vet* and *get*. Explain to children that nursery rhymes have a beat or rhythm. As you read the rhyme, emphasize the beat by clapping. Tell children to draw a picture of something that rhymes with the name of the picture in each row.

Name _____

Aa Bb Cc Dd Ee Ff Gg Hh Ii Jj Kk Ll Mm
Nn Oo Pp Qq Rr Ss Tt Uu Vv Ww Xx Yy Zz

Letter Recognition: Ss, Tt
Point to and say the uppercase and lowercase forms of the letter *Ss*. Tell children that the uppercase *S* is used if it's the first word in a sentence or the first letter in a person's name, such as *Sam*. Tell children to draw a line from the uppercase *S* to the lowercase *s* on the page. Repeat with the uppercase and lowercase letters *Tt* and the name *Tam*.

30 Grade K • Start Smart • Week 3

Name _____

Aa Bb Cc Dd Ee Ff Gg Hh Ii Jj Kk Ll Mm
Nn Oo Pp Qq Rr Ss Tt Uu Vv Ww Xx Yy Zz

Letter Recognition: *Uu, Vv*
Point to and say the uppercase and lowercase forms of the letter *Uu*. Tell children that the uppercase *U* is used if it's the first word in a sentence or the first letter in a person's name, such as *Uma*. Tell children to draw a line from the uppercase *U* to the lowercase *u* on the page. Repeat with the uppercase and lowercase letter *Vv* and the name *Vicky*.

Grade K • Start Smart • Week 3 **31**

Name _____

Aa Bb Cc Dd Ee Ff Gg Hh Ii Jj Kk Ll Mm
Nn Oo Pp Qq Rr Ss Tt Uu Vv Ww Xx Yy Zz

Letter Recognition: Ww, Xx
Point to and say the uppercase and lowercase forms of the letter *Ww*. Tell children that the uppercase letter *W* is used if it's the first word in a sentence or the first letter in a person's name, such as *Wendy*. Tell children to draw a line from each uppercase letter *W* to each lowercase *w*. Repeat with the uppercase and lowercase forms of the letter *Xx* and the name *Xing*.

Name _____

Aa Bb Cc Dd Ee Ff Gg Hh Ii Jj Kk Ll Mm
Nn Oo Pp Qq Rr Ss Tt Uu Vv Ww Xx Yy Zz

Letter Recognition: *Yy, Zz*
Point to and say the uppercase and lowercase forms of the letter *Yy*. Tell children that the capital letter *Y* is used if it's the first word in a sentence or the first letter in a person's name, such as *Yolanda*. Tell children to draw a line from each uppercase letter *Y* to each lowercase *y*. Repeat with the uppercase and lowercase forms of the letter *Zz* and the name *Zachary*. Then direct children's attention to the alphabet at the top of the page and say the name of each uppercase and lowercase letter. Then name random uppercase and lowercase letters and have children identify them.

Grade K • Start Smart • Week 3

Name _____

Aa Bb Cc Dd Ee Ff Gg Hh Ii Jj Kk Ll Mm
Nn Oo Pp Qq Rr Ss Tt Uu Vv Ww Xx Yy Zz

🍎   F   g   e   f   x

⭐   M   z   E   n   m

🌲   Q   o   q   b   c

🐟   S   t   c   o   s

Letter Identification Review
Review the alphabet with children. Then tell them to look at the uppercase letter in each row. Have children follow these directions:

🍎 Circle the lowercase *f*.   ⭐ Circle the lowercase *m*.
🌲 Circle the lowercase *q*.   🐟 Circle the lowercase *s*.

Have children take turns working with partners to identify the letters on the chart at the top of this page. Then guide children to turn to The Alphabet page on page 463. Have them identify all the uppercase letters, and then all the lowercase letters.

34   Grade K • Start Smart • Week 3

Name _____

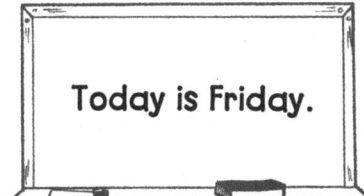

Category Words: Days of the Week
Explain to children that there are seven days of the week. Name the days: *Sunday, Monday, Tuesday, Wednesday, Thursday, Friday* and *Saturday*. Ask children how the days *Saturday* and *Sunday* are different from the other days of the week. Tell children that some of the pictures on this page show days of the week. Point to and name the pictures in each row. Have children circle the pictures that show days of the week. Have partners talk about what they do on Saturday and Sunday.

Grade K • Start Smart • Week 3

Name _____

| I | can |

_____ can ____ .

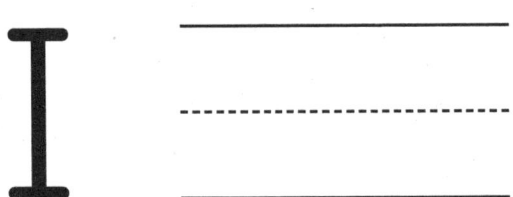 I _____ .

I _____ .

High-Frequency Words: *I, can*
Model the Read/Spell/Write routine with the words *I* and *can*. Have children choose a word from the box to complete each sentence. Have partners read the sentences to each other and talk about which of the things they can do on the page. Then say the words *I* and *can* for children to spell.

36 Grade K • Start Smart • Week 3

Name _____

I Can
give

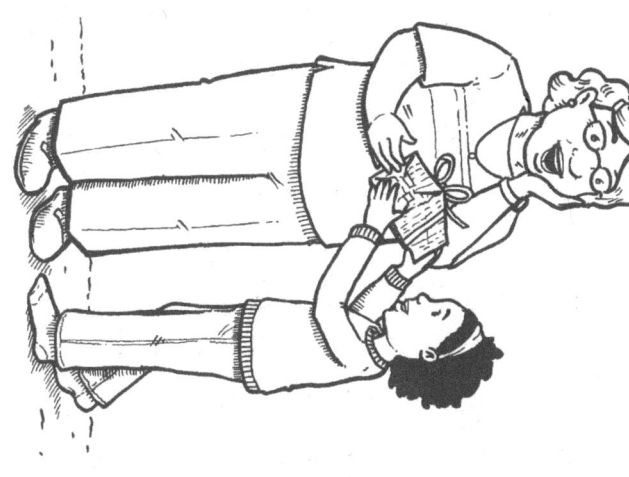

I can
give
!

Connect to Community
Encourage children to read the story to a family member or a friend.

Grade K • Start Smart • Week 3

4

I can
cut
.

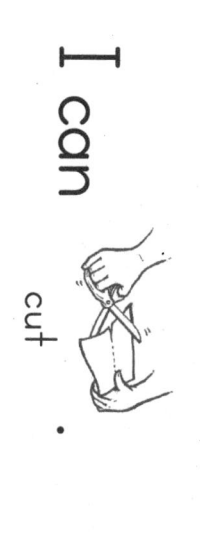

Review High-Frequency Words
Have children set a purpose for reading, such as finding out what the girl can do. Explain that words in a sentence are separated by spaces. Model pointing to the space between the words *I* and *can* on page 1. Then ask children to point to the space between the words *I* and *can* on page 3.

TEKS: K.(5)(A), K.(2)(D)(iii)

1

I can hide.

I can tie.

Name _____

Phonological Awareness: Sentence Segmentation
Explain to children that sentences are made up of words. Say: *I have a dog.* Tell children that there are four words in the sentence. Hold up a finger for each word in the sentence. Tell children you will color in four boxes to show that there are four words in the sentence. Then tell children to color in a box for each word that they hear in the following sentences: ★ *I did it!* 🌲 *Go now.* 🐟 *I like to read.*

Grade K • Unit 1 • Week 1 **39**

 Name _____

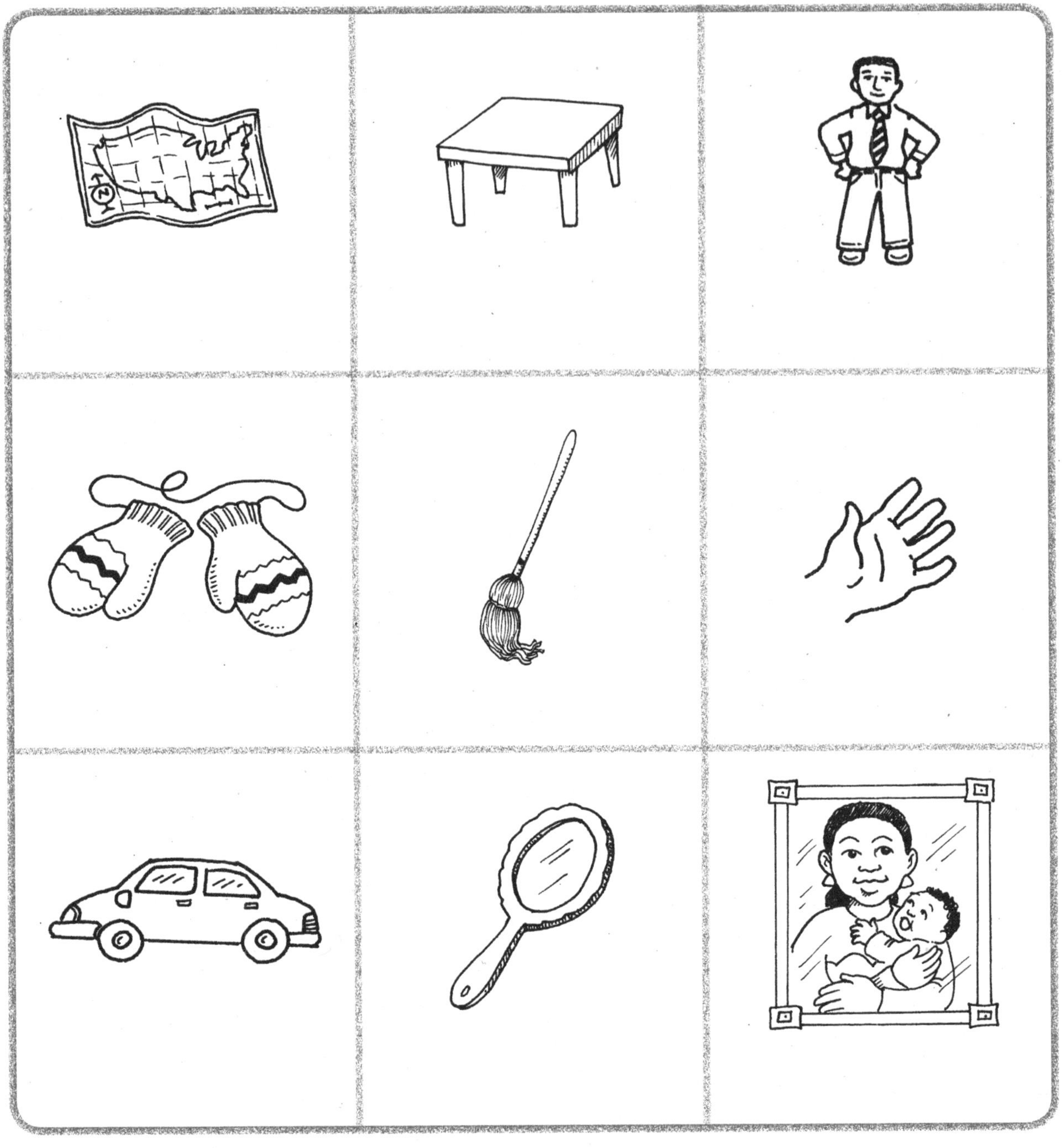

Phonemic Awareness: /m/
Point to and say the name of the picture of the map. Tell children that the word *map* begins with the /m/ sound. Have children repeat, *map*, /m/. Now point to and say the names of the rest of the pictures on the page. Tell children to circle the pictures that have names that begin with the /m/ sound as in *map*.

40 Grade K • Unit 1 • Week 1

Name _____

Phonemic Awareness: Phoneme Blending with /m/
Tell children to listen to the sounds in the word *mat*. Model blending the sounds to say the word *mat*, /mmmaaat/, *mat*. Have children repeat. Tell children you will draw a picture of a mat in the first box. Now have children listen as you say the sounds in some words. Have children repeat the sounds and blend them to say each word. Then have them draw a picture of the word in the box. Use these sounds: ★ /m//a//n/; 🌲 /p//a//d/; 🐟 /m//a//p/.

Grade K • Unit I • Week I

Name _____

Mm

Phonics: /m/m
Point to and say the name of the picture of the moon. Tell children that the word *moon* begins with the /m/ sound. Explain that the letter *m* stands for the /m/ sound. Now point to and say the names of the rest of the pictures on the page. Have children write the letter *m* next to the picture if its name begins with /m/ sound as in *moon*. Tell children to look at the pictures in each row from left to right.

42 Grade K • Unit I • Week I

Name _____

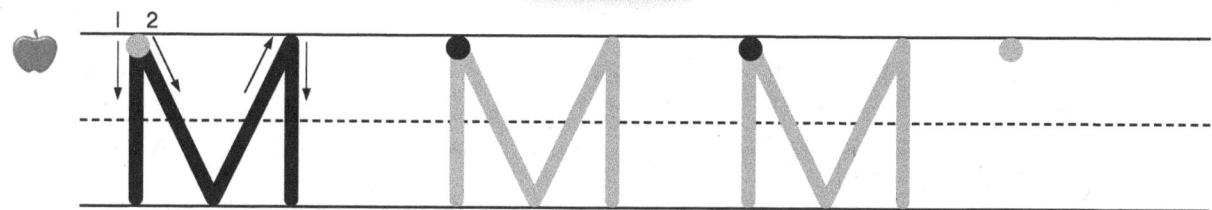

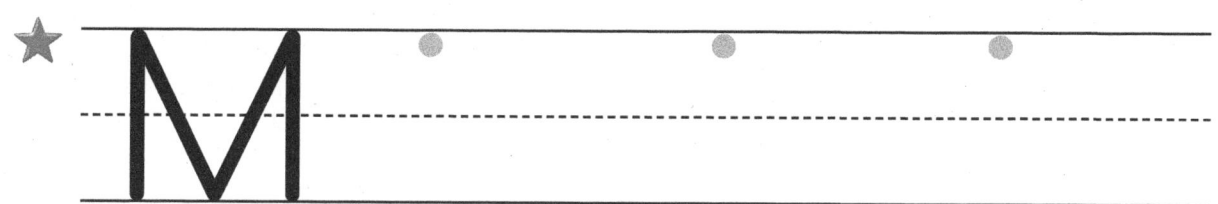

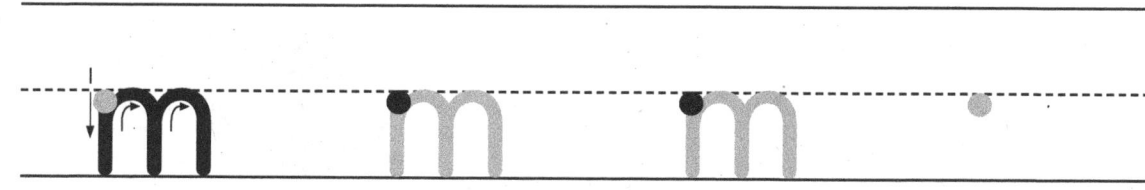

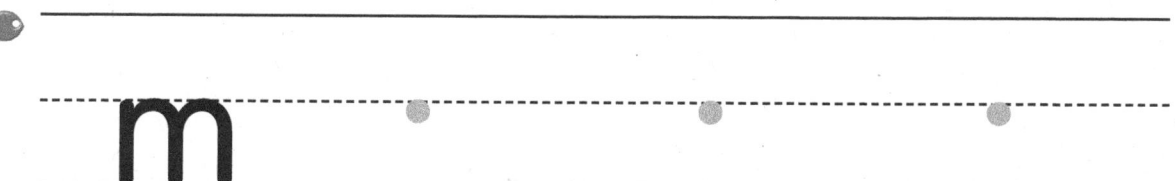

Handwriting: *Mm*
Demonstrate following the numbers and arrows to model for children the proper formation of the capital and lowercase *Mm*. To form the uppercase letter *M*, say: *Straight down. Go back to the top. Slant down. Slant up. Straight down.* For the lowercase *m*, say: *Straight down. Around and straight down. Around and straight down.* Have children use their finger to trace the models for the letter. Then have them write the uppercase and lowercase forms of the letter *Mm*.

Grade K • Unit 1 • Week 1 **43**

 Name _____

the

1. _____ 🌙

2. _____ 🧤

3. _____

4. _____ 🚕

High-Frequency Word: *the*
Model the Read/Spell/Write routine using the word *the*. Have children repeat. Point to and name the pictures. Then tell children to write the word *the* on each line and say the picture name. Have partners read the phrases. Then dictate the word *the* and have children spell and write the word.

Name _____

Category Words: Feeling Words
Explain that the words *happy, sad,* and *excited* are some words that describe feelings. Then name the pictures in each row. Have children circle the two pictures in each row that show feelings. Encourage children to use feeling words in sentences with a partner.

Grade K • Unit I • Week I **45**

Name _____

person　　place　　animal　　thing

- 🍎 The library is big.

- ⭐ The bird can fly.

- 🌲 The boy runs.

- 🐟 The fish swims.

Grammar: Singular Nouns
Point to and say the name of each picture at the top of the page. Explain to children that a noun is a word that names a person, place, animal, or thing. Tell children that *girl* is a noun that names a person; *library* is a noun that names a place or a location; *dog* is a noun that names an animal; *bike* is a noun that names a thing. Tell children to listen to each sentence. Have them circle the noun in each one and tell whether the noun names a person, a place, an animal, or a thing. Then encourage children to use nouns that name a person, a place, an animal, or a thing in sentences.

Name _____

🍎 The boy plants.

★ This store is new.

🌲 The nest is empty.

🐟 The wave is big.

Grammar: Singular Nouns
Remind children that a noun is a word that names a person, a place, an animal, or a thing. Say: *A girl names a person; the market names a place or location; a cat names an animal; and a ball names a thing.* Explain that nouns can name one person, place, animal or thing or more than one person, place, animal, or thing. Point to and say the names of the pictures on the page. Tell children to listen to each sentence, circle the noun and tell if it names one person, place, animal, or thing. Then tell children to refer back to a piece of writing that they did during the week and make sure they used nouns that name one person, place, animal or thing correctly.

Grade K • Unit 1 • Week 1   **47**

Name _____

🍎 i can see.

⭐ The man sees

🌲 the map is big.

🐟 Can you pat the dog.

Edit/Proofread
Read aloud the sentences. Tell children that a sentence begins with a capital letter and has an ending mark. Have children rewrite each sentence so it shows correct capitalization and end punctuation. Use gestures to clarify meaning when possible.

Name _____

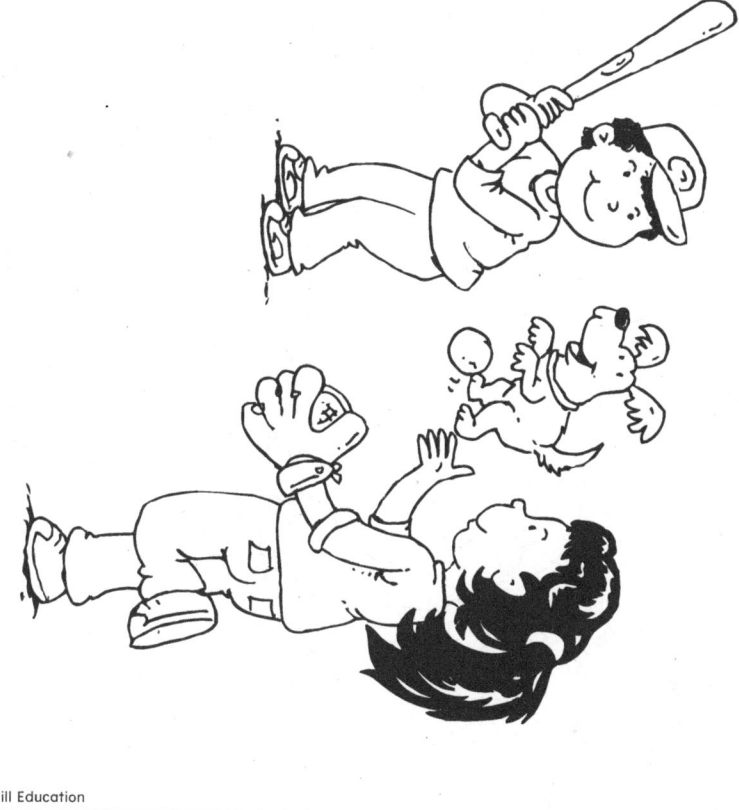

the friends

Connect to Community
Encourage children to read the story to a family member or a friend.

4 Grade K • Unit 1 • Week 1

The friends

the girl

High-Frequency Word: the
Have children set a purpose for reading, such as finding out about the friends. Then explain that a word is made up of letters. Say: *The word the is made up of three letters, t, h, and e.* Ask children to point to the word *the* on page 2, and then to a letter in the word.

TEKS: K.(5)(A), K.2(D)(iv)

1

the dog

the boy

Name _____

   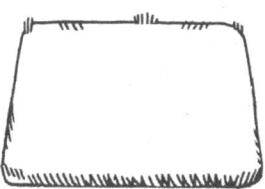

   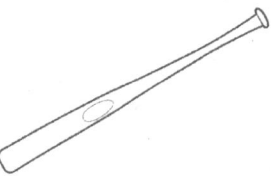

 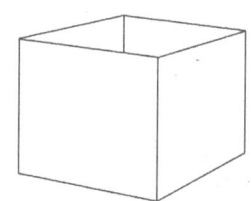  

 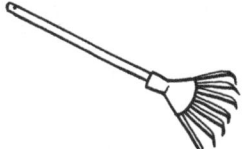 

Phonological Awareness: Recognize Rhyme
Explain to children that words that rhyme have the same ending sounds. Point to and name the pictures in the first row: *man, can, mat*. Say: *The words* man *and* can *rhyme because they have the same ending sounds.* They end with the sounds /an/. Tell children you will circle these pictures. Now point to and say the names of the other pictures on the page. Have children circle the two pictures in each row that have names that rhyme.

Grade K • Unit 1 • Week 2 **51**

 Name _____

Phonemic Awareness: /a/
Point to and say the name of the picture of the ant. Tell children that the word *ant* begins with the /a/ sound. Have children repeat, *ant*, /a/. Now point to and say the names of the rest of the pictures on the page. Tell children to circle the pictures that have names that begin with the /a/ sound as in *ant*.

52 Grade K • Unit I • Week 2

Name _____

Phonemic Awareness: Phoneme Blending with /a/
Tell children to listen to the sounds in the word *at*. Model blending the sounds to say the word *at*, /aaat/, *at*. Point out your mouth position for each sound. Have children repeat. Then tell children you will say the sounds in more words. Have them blend the sounds to say each word. Then have them draw a picture of the word: 🍎 /m//a//n/; ★ /c//a//t/; 🌲 /k//a//p/; 🐟 /d//a//d/.

Grade K • Unit I • Week 2 53

 Name _____

 ------  ------

 ------ ------

------  ------

------  ------

Phonics: /a/ a
Point to and say the name of the picture of the apple. Tell children that the word *apple* begins with the /a/ sound. Explain that the letter *a* stands for the /a/ sound. Now point to and say the names of the rest of the pictures on the page. Have children write the letter *a* next to the picture if its name begins with the /a/ sound as in *apple*. Tell children to look at the pictures in each row from left to right. Then tell them to work their way from the top of the page to the bottom.

54 Grade K • Unit I • Week 2

Name _____

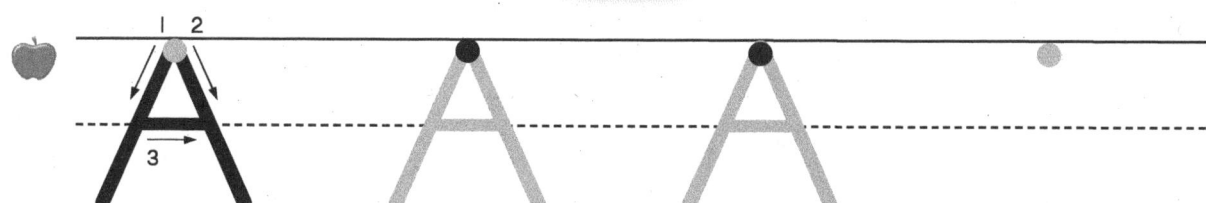

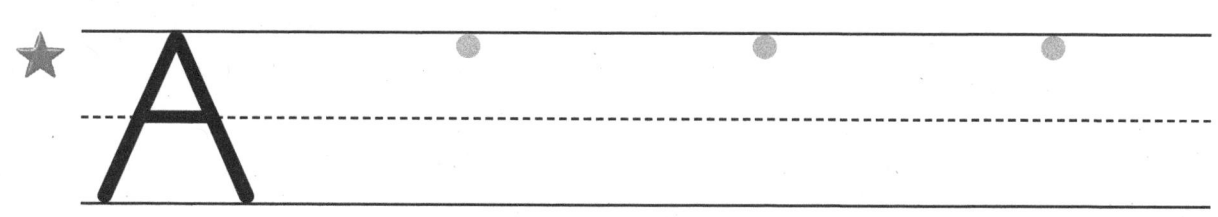

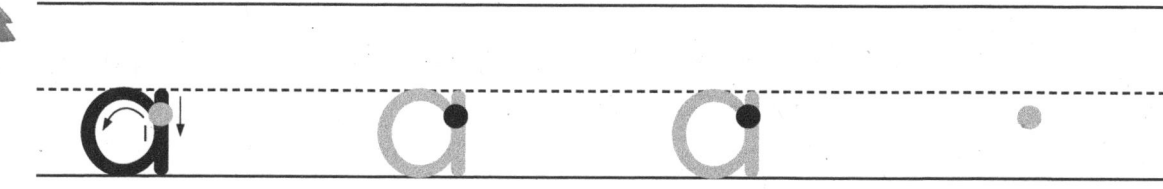

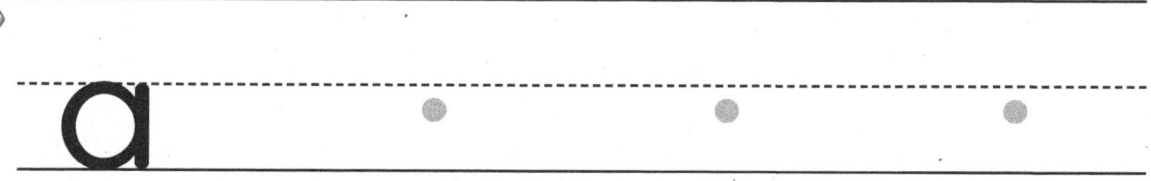

Handwriting: *Aa*
Demonstrate following the numbers and arrows to model the proper formation of the uppercase and lowercase *Aa*. To form the uppercase letter *A* say: *Slant down. Go back to the top. Slant down. Straight across the dotted line.* To form the lowercase letter *a* say: *Circle back, then around. Straight down.* Have children use their finger to trace the models for the letters. Then have them write the uppercase and lowercase forms of the letters *Aa*.

Grade K • Unit I • Week 2

Name _____

| we   can |

_____
🍎 _____ can build.

_____
★ We _____ play.

_____
🌲 _____ can dance.

High-Frequency Words: *we, can*
Model the Read/Spell/Write routine with the word *we*. Have children repeat the routine using the words *we* and *can*. Then have children write a word from the box on each line to complete the sentences. Have partners read the sentences to each other. Then dictate the words *we* and *can* for children to spell.

Name _____

Category Words: Family Words
Explain to children that different people make up a family. Words like *mother, father, sister,* and *brother* are words we can use to tell about families. Then point to and name the pictures in each row. Have children circle the two pictures in each row that show who could belong in a family.

Grade K • Unit I • Week 2 **57**

 Name _____

cat   bus   cheese

🍎 The chair is soft.

⭐ The egg is white.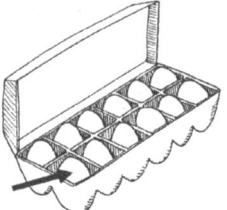

🌲 The kite flies high.

🐟 A grape is sweet.

Grammar: Singular Nouns
Remind children that a noun names a person, place, animal, or thing. Point to and name the pictures at the top of the page. Tell children that these are pictures of nouns that name one animal or thing. Then read each sentence and say the names of the pictures. Tell children to circle the noun in each sentence. Then tell children to refer back to a piece of writing that they did during the week and make sure they used nouns that name one animal or thing correctly.

58 Grade K • Unit 1 • Week 2

Name _____

🍎 I pet the _____.
            dog   big

⭐ My _____ is nice.
     ran   mom

🌲 The _____ is tall.
      tree   like

🐟 The _____ is pretty.
      jumps   girl

Grammar: Nouns
Read the sentences and word choices. Point to and say the name of each picture. Then tell children to write the word that completes each sentence on the lines. Use gestures to clarify meaning.

Grade K • Unit I • Week 2   **59**

Name _____

🍎 i see it.

⭐ Can I sit.

🌲 I can nap

🐟 We can go?

Edit/Proofread
Tell children to listen as you read aloud the sentences. Have them rewrite each sentence so it shows correct capitalization and punctuation. Use gestures to clarify meaning.

Name _____

We Can!

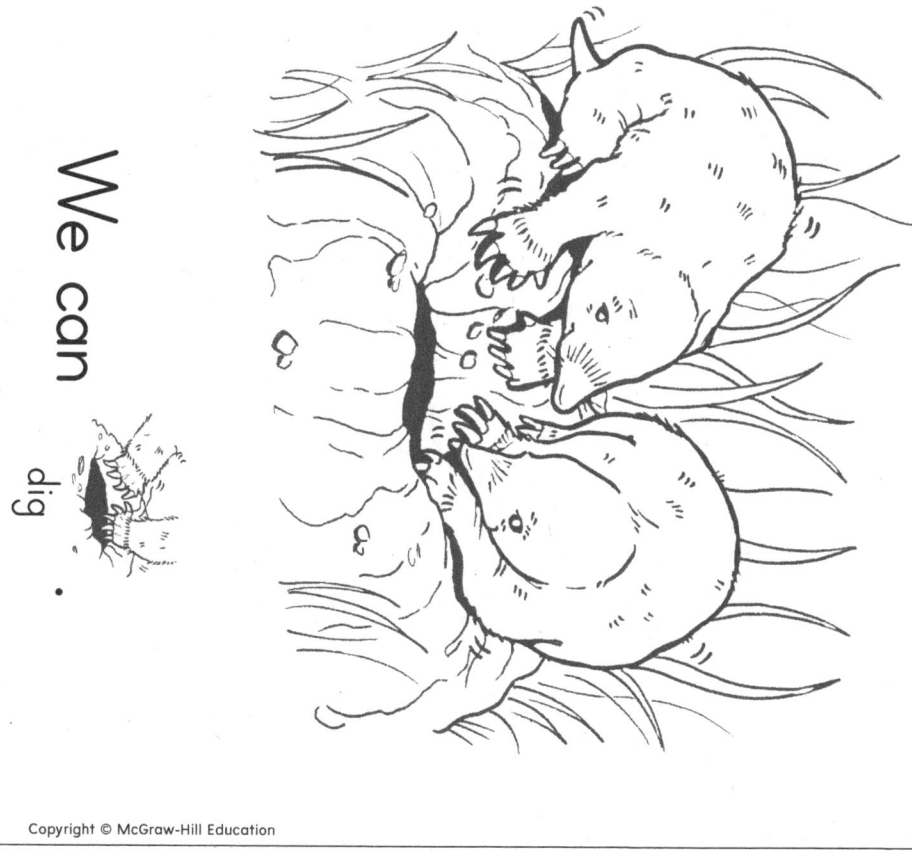

We can hop.

High-Frequency Words: we
Have children set a purpose for reading, such as finding out about what the different animals do. Explain that each word in a sentence is separated from the next word by a space. Point to the space between the words *We* and *can* on page 1. Then ask children to point to the space between the words *we* and *can* on page 3 of the story.

TEKS: K.(5)(A), K.(2)(D)(iii)

1

We can dig.

Connect to Community
Encourage children to read the story to a family member or a friend.

4 Grade K • Unit 1 • Week 2

We can fly!

We can run.

Name _____

Phonological Awareness: Onset and Rime Blending
Explain to children that words are made up of beginning and ending sounds. Say the word *sit*. Now say /s/ followed by /it/. Blend the sounds to say *sit*. Have children repeat, /s/ /it/, /sit/, *sit*. Tell children that you will draw a picture of a person sitting in the first box. Then say the beginning and ending sounds in some other words. Tell children to blend the sounds to say the word. Have children draw a picture in each box that shows the picture name. ★ /s//ad/, *sad* 🌲 /m//at/, *mat* 🐟 /s//un/, *sun*.

Grade K • Unit I • Week 3

 Name _____

Phonemic Awareness: /s/
Point to and say the name of the picture of the number six. Tell children that the word *six* begins with the /s/ sound. Have children repeat, *six*, /s/. Now point to and say the names of the rest of the pictures on the page. Tell children to circle the pictures that have names that begin with the /s/ sound as in *six*.

64 Grade K • Unit I • Week 3

Name _____

🍎	★
🌲	🐟

Phonemic Awareness: Phoneme Blending with /s/
Tell children to listen to the sounds in the word *sit*. Model blending the sounds to say the word *sit*, /sssiiit/, *sit*. Have children repeat. Then tell children you will say the sounds in more words. Have them blend the sounds to say each word. Then have them draw a picture of the word: 🍎 /s//a//d/; ★ /s//u//n/; 🌲 /s//i//p/; 🐟 /s//a//m/.

Name _____

Phonics: /s/s
Point to the first picture and say the word *sun*. Tell children that the word *sun* begins with the /s/ sound. Explain that the letter *s* stands for /s/. Now point to and say the name of each picture. Have children write the letter *s* next to the picture if its name begins with /s/ as in *sun*. Remind children to look at the pictures in each row from left to right and to work their way from the top to the bottom of the page.

66 Grade K • Unit 1 • Week 3

Name _____

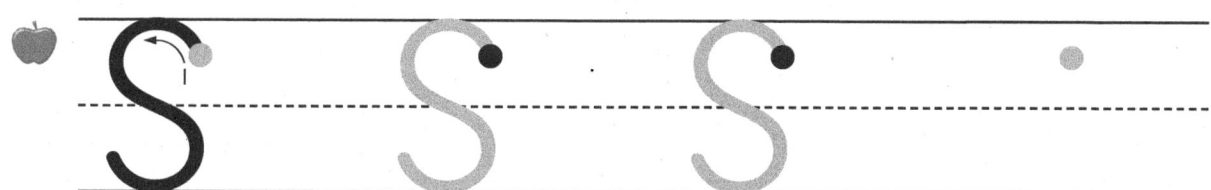

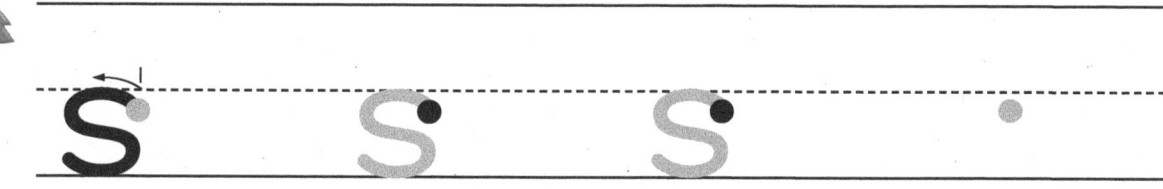

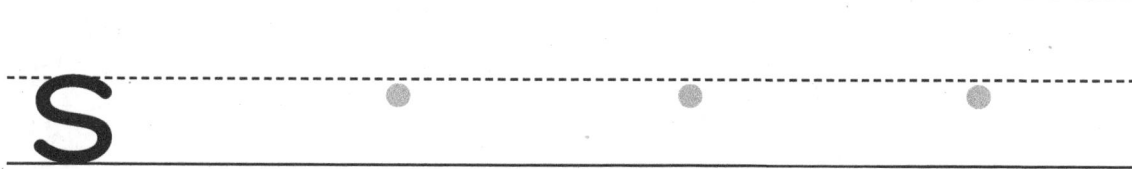

Handwriting: *Ss*
Demonstrate following the numbers and arrows to model for children the proper formation of the uppercase and lowercase letters *Ss*. To form the uppercase letter *S* say: *Circle back, sweep around, and back again.* To form the lowercase letter *s* say: *Circle back, sweep around, and back again.* Have children use their finger to trace the models for the letters. Then have them write the uppercase and lowercase forms of the letters *Ss*.

Grade K • Unit I • Week 3 **67**

Name _____

| see   the |

🍎 We _____ the ____ .

⭐ We _____ the ____ .

🌲 I can see _____ .

🐟 I can see _____ .

High-Frequency Words: *see, the*
Model the Read/Spell/Write routine with the word *see*. Have children repeat the routine using the words *see* and *the*. Then have them write a word from the box on the line to complete each sentence. Have partners read the sentences to each other. Then dictate *see* and *the* for children to spell.

Grade K • Unit 1 • Week 3

Name _____

  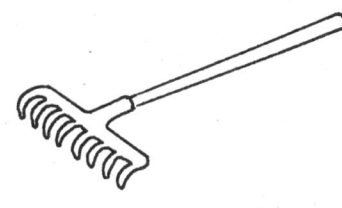

Category Words: Sensory Words
Explain that people use their senses to experience things. Say that there are five senses. Say that seeing, hearing, smelling, tasting, and touching are all senses. Point to and name the pictures in each row. Discuss how people are using their senses. Have children circle the two pictures in each row that show people using their senses.

 Name _____

home   classroom   town

🍎 The store is open.

⭐ The library is quiet.

🌲 The field is big.

🐟 The beach is hot.

Grammar: Nouns
Remind children that a noun names a person, a place, an animal or a thing. Point to and name the pictures at the top of the page. Explain that these are all nouns that name places. Then read each sentence and point to and name the picture. Tell children to circle the noun in each sentence.

Name _____

🍎 My _____ grows.
      house   plant

⭐ The _____ is warm.
      pool   mitten

🌲 The _____ sails.
      water   boat

🐟 The _____ helps animals.
      table   vet

Grammar: Nouns
Remind children that a noun names a person, a place, an animal or a thing. Then read each sentence and the two answer choices. Point to and name the pictures. Tell children to write the noun that best completes each sentence on the line.

Name _____

🍎 You and i can hop.

⭐ Can I sit.

🌲 i sat with Sam.

🐟 we can walk to school.

Edit/Proofread
Tell children to listen as you read aloud the sentences. Have them rewrite each sentence so it shows correct capitalization and punctuation. Use gestures to clarify meaning.

Name _____

I see

I see the ____.
worm

High-Frequency Words: see
Have children set a purpose for reading, such as finding out what the children see. Then point out that reading moves from left to right. Have children demonstrate moving their finger from left to right as they read.

1

We see the ____.
garden

Connect to Community
Encourage children to read the story to a family member or a friend.

4 Grade K · Unit 1 · Week 3

TEKS: K.(5)A), K.(2)(D)(ii)

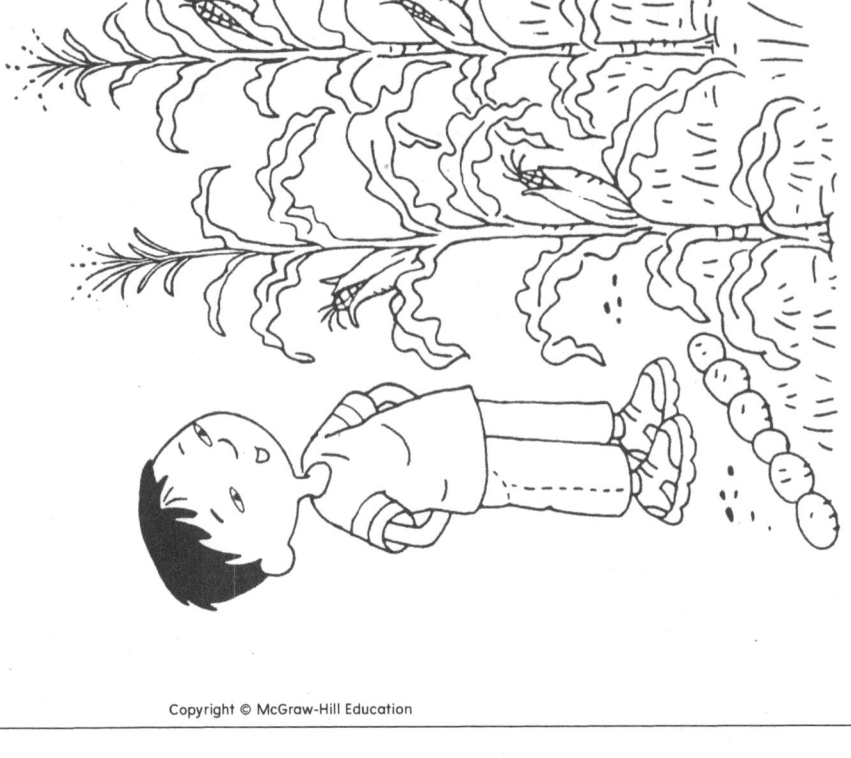

I see the  corn.

I see the  pumpkin.

Name _____

Phonological Awareness: Alliteration
Explain to children that sometimes words in a sentence begin with the same sound. Read the following sentence aloud: *Sebastian sells socks.* Ask children to name the sound that all of the words begin with: /s/. Now say the following sentence aloud: *Mason eats lunch.* Ask children if the words in this sentence begin with the same sound. Explain that you will read more sentences; some will have words that begin with the same sound and some will not. Read the following sentences and have children draw a picture of the sentence when they hear words with the same sound. 🍎 *Tom taps the turtle.* ★ *Becky bounces a ball.* 🌲 *Maya plays outside.* 🐟 *Liam likes lollipops.*

Grade K • Unit 2 • Week 1   **75**

 Name _____

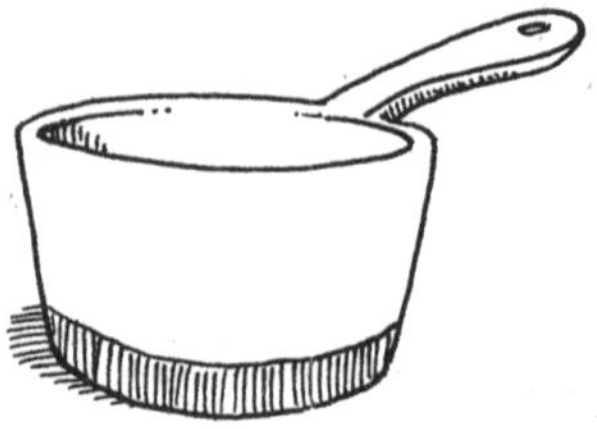

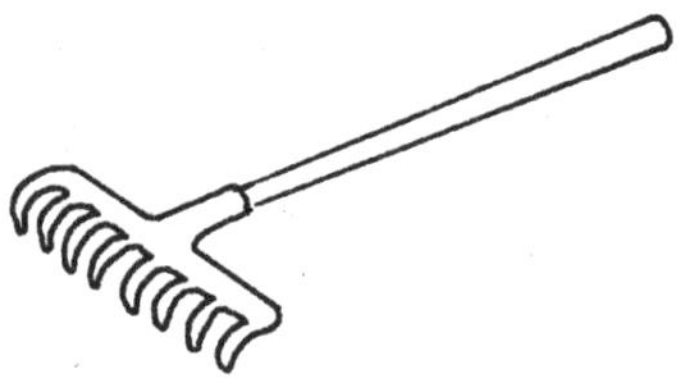

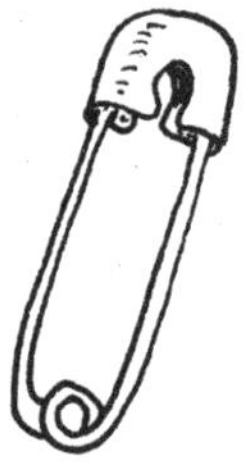

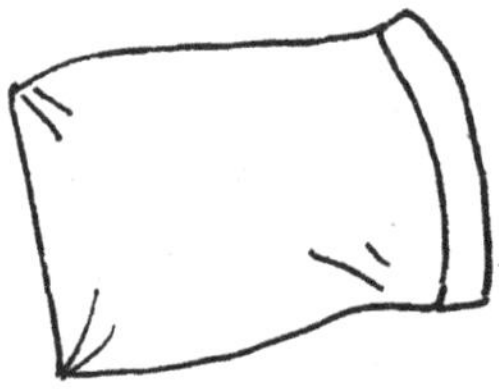

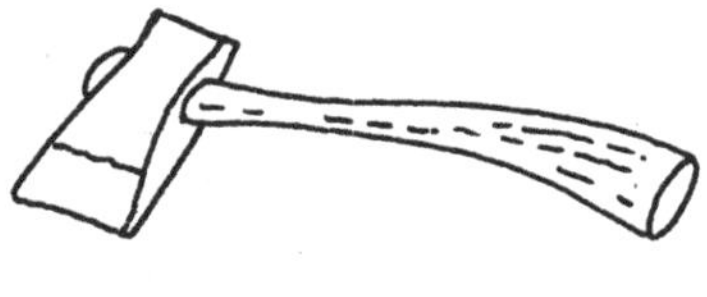

Phonemic Awareness: /p/
Point to and say the name of the picture of the pen in the first box and explain that *pen* begins with the /p/ sound. Have children repeat, *pen*, /p/. Then point to and say the names of the rest of the pictures on the page. Tell children to circle the pictures that have names that begin with the /p/ sound as in *pen*.

76 Grade K • Unit 2 • Week 1

Name _____

Phonemic Awareness: Phoneme Blending with /p/
Tell children to listen to the sounds in the word *pop*. Model blending the sounds to say the word *pop*, /pooop/, *pop*. Have children repeat. Then tell children you will say the sounds in more words. Have them blend the sounds to say each word. Then have them draw a picture of the word: 🍎 /p//a//n/; ⭐ /p//i//g/; 🌲 /p//e//t/; 🐟 /p//o//t/.

Grade K • Unit 2 • Week 1

Name _____

Pp

Phonics: /p/p
Point to and say the word *pen* in the apple row. Say that it begins with the /p/ sound. Explain that the letter *p* stands for the /p/ sound. Now point to and say the names of the rest of the pictures. Have children write the letter *p* next to the picture if its name begins with the /p/ sound. Remind children to look at the pictures in each row from left to right and to work their way from the top to the bottom of the page.

78 Grade K • Unit 2 • Week 1

Name _____

sap   am   map

Phonics/Spelling
Decode Words: Say *am* and point to your mouth position. Repeat with *Pam*. Write both words and model how to decode them. Then have children decode the words at the top of the page. **Spell Words:** Have children write the word that names each picture. Then dictate the words *am* and *sap* for children to spell. Model how to spell *am* by writing a letter for each sound. Then decode the word.

Grade K • Unit 2 • Week 1 **79**

Name _____

p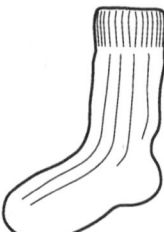

a

m

s

Phonics: Letter/Sound Match
Point to the *p* and explain to children that this letter stands for the /p/ sound. Model drawing a line from the letter *p* to the picture of the pan. Then say the name of each picture. Tell children to draw a line from each letter to the picture whose name begins with that letter and sound.

80 Grade K • Unit 2 • Week 1

Name _____

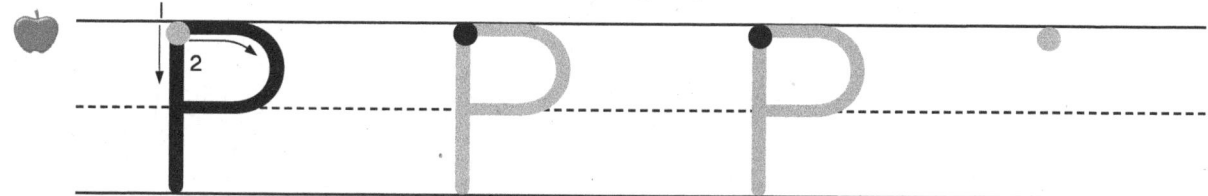

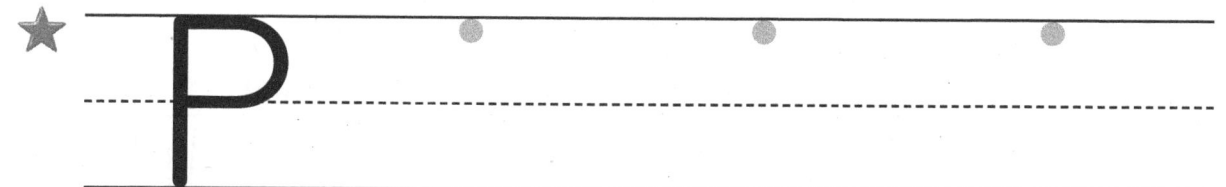

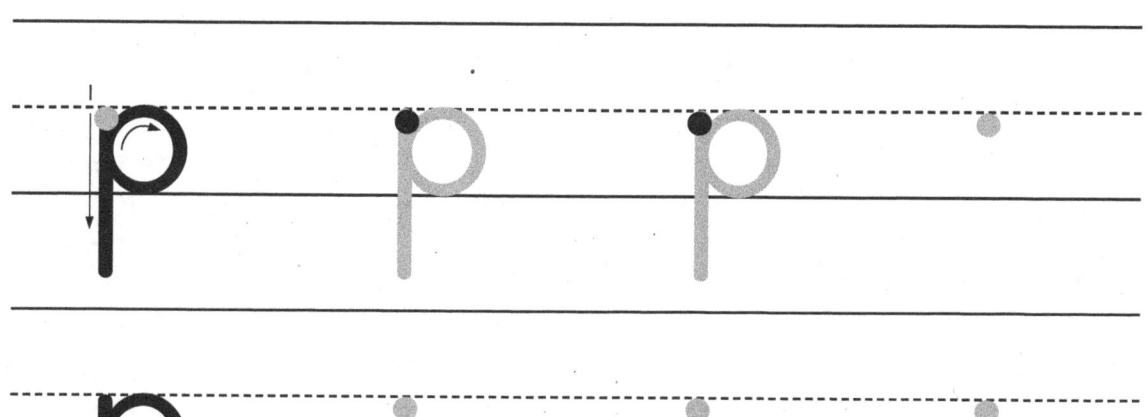

Handwriting: *Pp*
Demonstrate following the numbers and arrows to model for children the proper formation of the uppercase and lowercase *Pp*. To form the uppercase letter *P* say: *Straight down. Go back to the top. Around and in at the dotted line.* To form the lowercase letter *p* say: *Straight down, past the bottom line. Circle around all the way.* Have children use their finger to trace the models for each of the letters. Then have them write the uppercase and lowercase forms of the letters *Pp*.

Grade K • Unit 2 • Week 1 **81**

 Name _____

| a   see |

_____

🍎 We _____ a  .

_____

⭐ We see _____  .

_____

🌲 I can see _____  .

_____

🐟 I can _____ a  .

High-Frequency Words: *a, see*
Model the Read/Spell/Write routine with the word *a*. Have children repeat. Remind them that the other word in the box is *see*. Have children write a word from the box on the line to complete each sentence. Have partners read the sentences to each other. Then dictate the words *a* and *see* for children to spell.

Name _____

Category Words: Colors
Explain that there are many colors. Say: *Red, green, yellow, and orange are colors.* Then say: *A tomato and a strawberry are red.* Then point to and name the pictures in each row. Have children circle the two pictures in each row that are the same color. Have partners tell what other things are the same color.

Grade K • Unit 2 • Week 1   **83**

Name _____

sits jumps stops helps

🍎 The boy _____ on the chair.

⭐ The girl _____ high.

🌲 The car _____ .

🐟 The vet _____ animals.

Grammar: Verbs
Explain to children that a verb is a word that shows an action. Point to and say the four verbs in the box. Read the first sentence. Tell children you will choose a word from the box to complete the sentence. Then write the word *sits* on the line. Then read each of the other sentences and talk about the pictures. Help children choose a word from the box to complete each sentence.

84 Grade K • Unit 2 • Week 1

Name _____

🍎 The girl _____.

      swims   book

⭐ Tim _____ fast.

      fast   runs

🌲 The dog _____ its tail.

      wags   cute

🐟 The baby _____.

      loud   crawls

Grammar: Verbs
Remind children that a verb is a word that shows an action. Say: *The word* jumps *is a verb because it tells about an action*. Encourage children to name different actions they make. Then point to and name the pictures on the page. Read each sentence and the two answer choices. Tell children to write the verb that completes each sentence. Tell children to refer back to a piece of writing that they did during the week and make sure they used verbs correctly.

Name _____

🍎 Isee a pie.

⭐ We see a pig

🌲 my brother tim is tall.

🐟 we like the dog.

Edit/Proofread
Tell children to listen as you read aloud the sentences. Remind children that a sentence begins with a capital letter and ends with a punctuation mark, such as a period. Also remind them that a person's name begins with a capital letter, and the word *I* is always a capital letter. Have them rewrite each sentence so it shows correct capitalization, spacing, and end punctuation.

86 Grade K • Unit 2 • Week I

Name _____

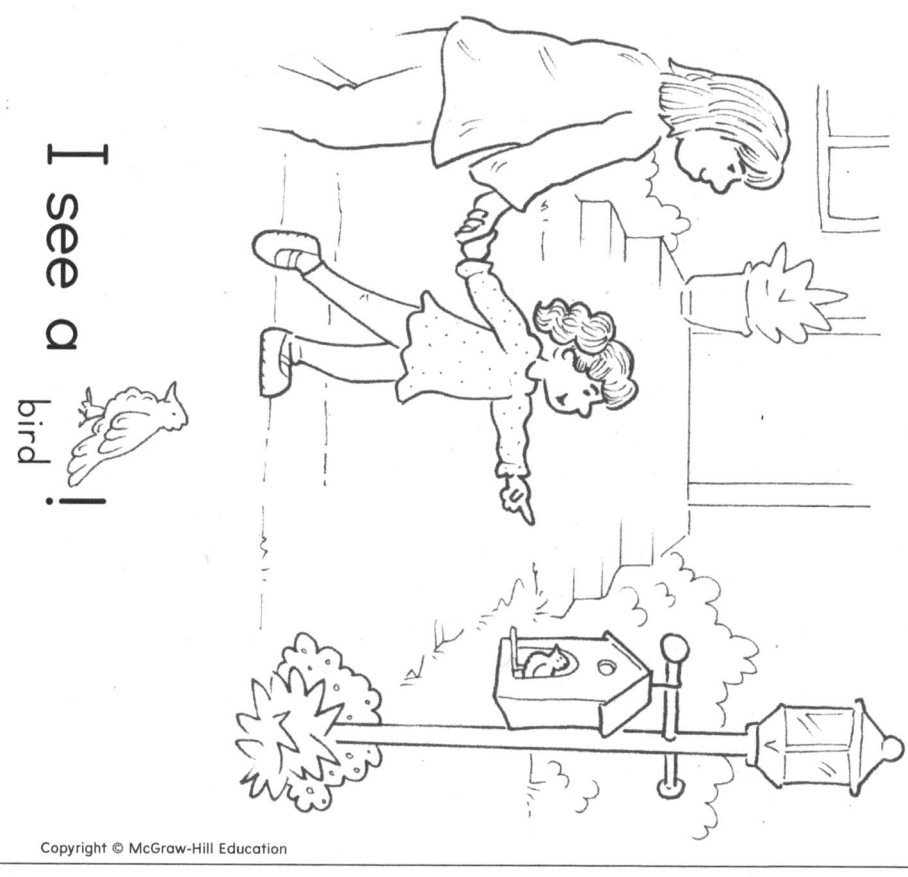

I see a ￼ bird !

Connect to Community
Encourage children to read the story to a family member or a friend.

4

Grade K • Unit 2 • Week 1

A
Walk

I see a ￼ bird .

High-Frequency Words: *a*
Have children set a purpose for reading such as finding out what the little girl sees. Point to the space between each word on page 1. Then encourage children to point to the space between each word on page 3.

TEKS: K.(5)(A), K.(2)(D)(iii)

1

I see a 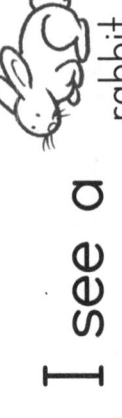 rabbit.

I see a 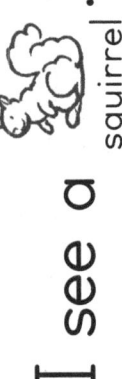 squirrel.

Name _____

Phonological Awareness: Onset and Rime Blending
Say the word tap. Then say /t/ /ap/, tap. Have children repeat. Explain that you first said the very beginning sound in the word tap and then you said the remaining sounds. Tell children that you will say the beginning and ending sounds in some words. Tell them to blend the beginning and ending sounds together to say the word. Then tell children to draw a picture of the word in each box. 🍎 /m//at/, mat; ★ /t//ub/, tub; 🌲 /m//op, mop; 🐟 /h//at/, hat.

Grade K • Unit 2 • Week 2

Name _____

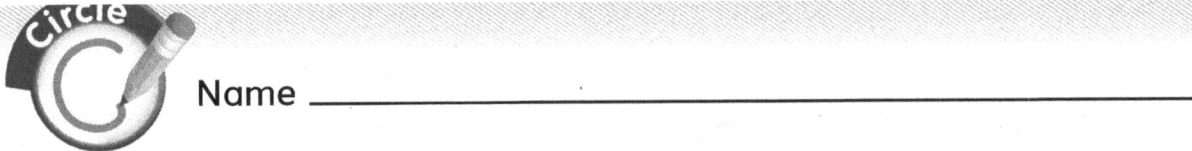

Phonemic Awareness: /t/
Point to and say the name of the picture of the tomato in the first box and explain that *tomato* begins with the /t/ sound. Have children repeat, *tomato*, /t/. Then point to and say the name of each picture on the page. Tell children to circle the pictures in each row that have names that begin with the /t/ sound.

90 Grade K • Unit 2 • Week 2

Name _____

Phonemic Awareness: Phoneme Blending with /t/
Tell children to listen to the sounds in the word *tip*. Model blending the sounds to say the word *tip*, /tiiip/, *tip*. Have children repeat. Then tell children you will say the sounds in more words. Have them blend the sounds to say each word. Then have them draw a picture of the word: 🍎 /t//e//n/; ★ /c//a//t/; 🌲 /t//u//b/; 🐟 /t//o//p/.

Grade K • Unit 2 • Week 2   91

Name _____

Phonics: /t/t
Point to and say the word *tie*. Tell children that *tie* begins with the /t/ sound. Explain that the letter *t* stands for the /t/ sound. Now point to and say the names of the rest of the pictures. Have children write the letter *t* next to the picture if its name begins with the /t/ sound as in *tie*. Remind children to look at the pictures in each row from left to right and to work their way from the top to the bottom of the page.

Name _____

Tam am tap at
_____

 _____
- -
_____

 _____
- -
_____

Phonics/Spelling
Decode Words: Say *am* and point to your mouth position. Repeat with *Sam*. Write both words and model how to decode them. Then have children decode the words at the top of the page. **Spell Words:** Then have children write the word that names the first picture. Tell children that they should then write a word that begins with /t/ that tells a girl's name. Say aloud the words *at, am,* and *sap* for children to spell.

Grade K • Unit 2 • Week 2   **93**

Name _____

t

a

m

p

Phonics: Letter/Sound Match
Point to the letter *t* and explain to children that this letter stands for the /t/ sound. Model drawing a line from the letter *t* to the picture of the turtle. Then say the name of each picture and tell children to draw a line from each letter to the picture whose name begins with that letter and sound.

Name _____

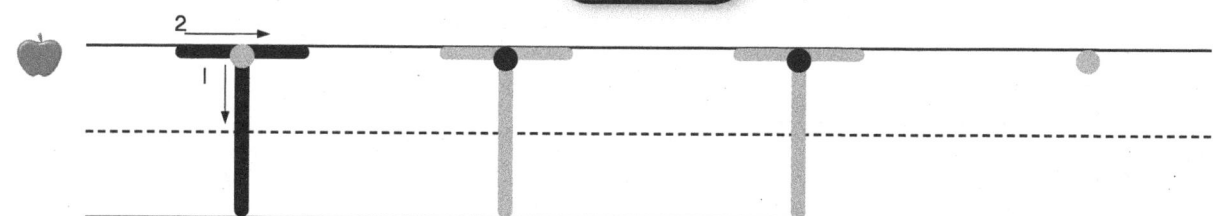

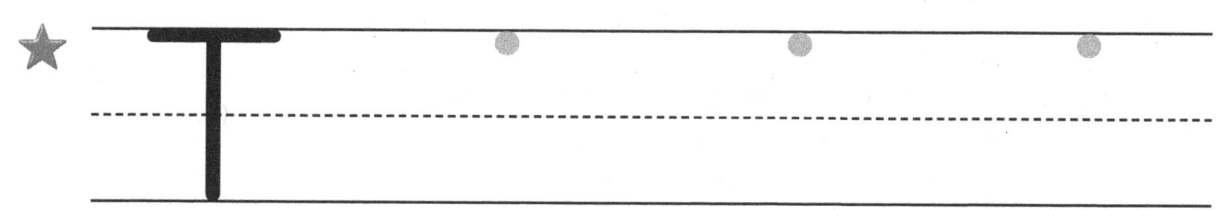

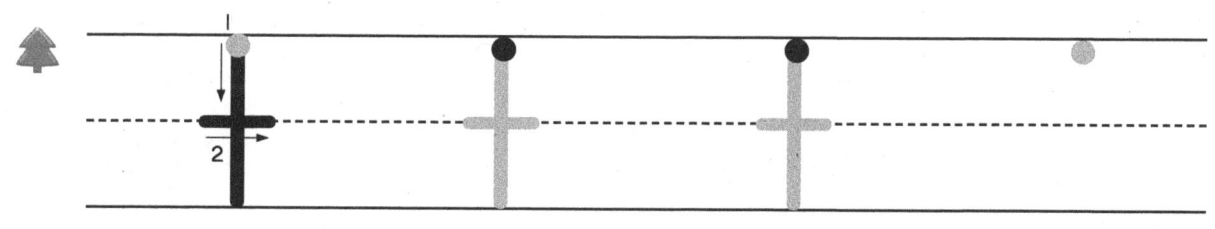

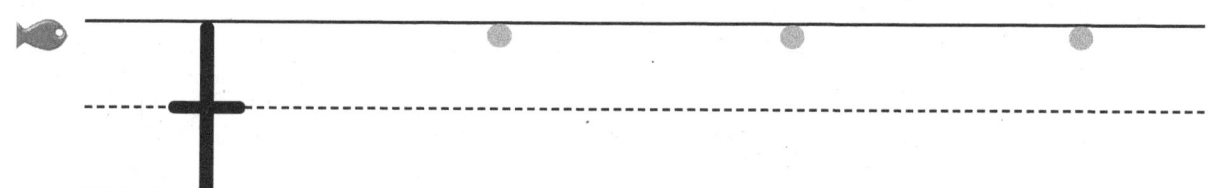

Handwriting: *Tt*
Demonstrate following the numbers and arrows to model for children the proper formation of the uppercase and lowercase *Tt*. To form the uppercase letter *T* say: *Straight down. Go back to the top. Straight across.* To form the lowercase letter *t* say: *Straight down. Go to the dotted line. Straight across.* Have children use their finger to trace the models for each of the letters. Then have them write the uppercase and lowercase forms of the letters *Tt*.

Grade K • Unit 2 • Week 2 **95**

 Name _____

| like   a |

_____

- - - - - - - - - - - - - - - -

🍎 I _____ a    red .

_____

- - - - - - - - - - - - - - - -

⭐ I like _____ .

_____

- - - - - - - - - - - - - - - -

🌲 I _____ a    .

_____

- - - - - - - - - - - - - - - -

🐟 I _____ .    .

High-Frequency Words: *like, a*
Model the Read/Spell/Write routine with *like*. Have children repeat the routine using the words *like* and *a*. Then have children write a word from the box on the line to complete each sentence. Have partners read the sentences to each other. Dictate the words *like* and *a* for children to spell.

96 Grade K • Unit 2 • Week 2

Name _____

  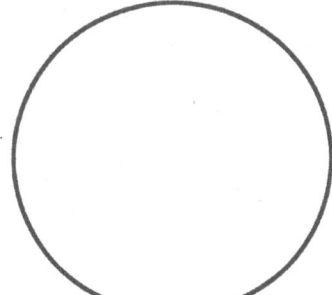 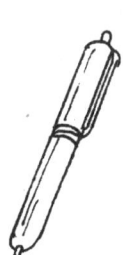

 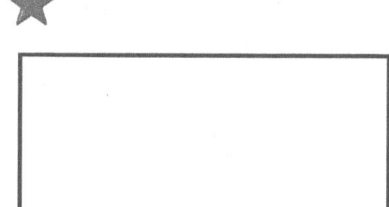  

 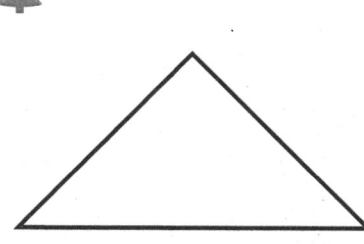  

Category Words: Shapes
Explain to children that things can be different shapes, such as a circle, square, triangle, or rectangle. Tell children that some of the pictures on this page show different shapes. Point to and name the pictures in each row. Have children circle the two pictures in each row that show shapes. Encourage children to use shape words in sentences with a partner.

Name _____

🍎 The lion walks.

⭐ We dance.

🌲 I draw on the paper.

🐟 Pam plays with the dog.

Grammar: Verbs
Remind children that a verb is a word that names an action. Say: *The word* jump *is a verb*. Then read each sentence and point to and name the pictures. Tell children to circle the verb in each sentence. Then encourage children to refer back to a piece of writing that they did during the week and make sure they used verbs correctly.

Name _____

🍎 The boy _____.

swims   water

★ The tiger _____.

growls   sleeps

🌲 The man _____.

jumps   hikes

🐟 The girl _____.

jumps   cute

Grammar: Verbs
Remind children that a verb tells about an action. Point to and name the pictures on the page. Then read each sentence and the two answer choices. Tell children to write the verb that completes each sentence.

Name _____

🍎 pam can see Sam.

⭐ Can I see pam?

🌲 Max can mix it

🐟 Tam can find it?

Edit/Proofread
Tell children to listen as you read aloud the sentences. Have them rewrite each sentence so it shows correct capitalization and end punctuation.

Name _____

We Like!

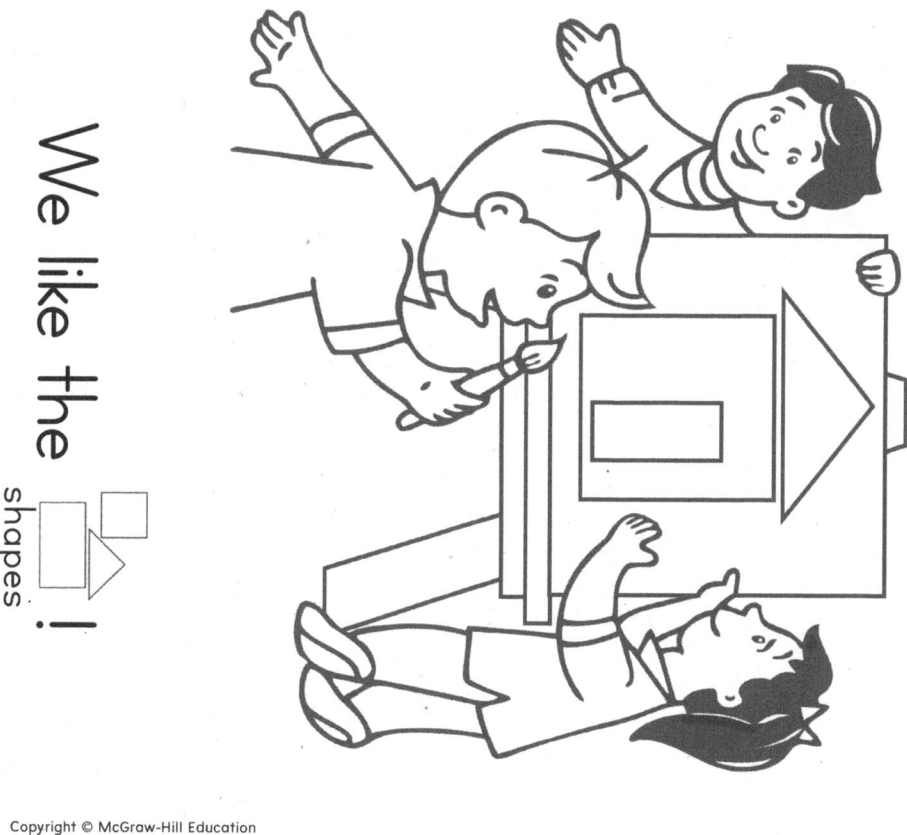

I like the ☐ !
       square

High-Frequency Words
Have children set a purpose for reading, such as to find out what the children like. Point to the space between each word on page 1. Then encourage children to point to the space between each word on page 3.

TEKS: K.(5)(A), K.(2)(D)(iii)

1

We like the 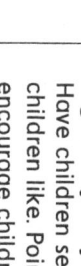 !
       shapes

Connect to Community
Encourage children to read the story to a family member or a friend.

4   Grade K • Unit 2 • Week 2

Copyright © McGraw-Hill Education

I like the ▭ rectangle.

3

I like the △ triangle.

2

Name _____

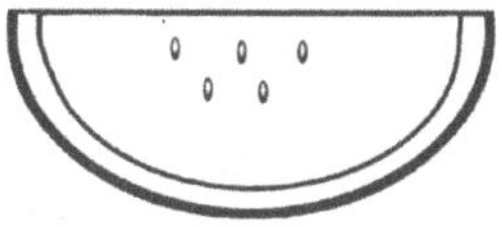

Phonological Awareness: Count and Pronounce Syllables
Point to the pineapple and say its name. Model clapping for each syllable or part in the word. Point out that there are three parts or syllables in *pineapple*. Tell children that you will write the number 3 in the box because *pineapple* has three parts or syllables. Point to and name the picture in each row. Tell children to write a number on the line to show how many parts or syllables they hear. Then have children identify the syllables or word parts in each word.

Grade K • Unit 2 • Week 3

Review Phonics: /m/m, /a/a, /p/p, /s/s, /t/t
Point to and say the word *ant*. Tell children that *ant* begins with the /a/ sound. Explain that the letter *a* stands for the /a/ sound. Review the /m/, /p/, /s/, and /t/ sounds. Now point to and say the names of the rest of the pictures on the page. Have children write the letter that stands for the first sound in the picture name on the lines. Remind children to look at the pictures in each row from left to right and work their way from the top of the page to the bottom.

Name _____

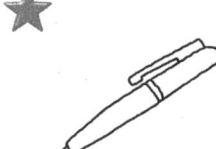 _ _ _ _ _ _ _ _    _ _ _ _ _ _ _ _

 _ _ _ _ _ _ _ _   _ _ _ _ _ _ _ _

 _ _ _ _ _ _ _ _    _ _ _ _ _ _ _ _

 _ _ _ _ _ _ _ _    _ _ _ _ _ _ _ _

Review Phonics: /m/m, /a/a, /p/p, /s/s, /t/t
Point to and say the name of each picture on the page. Then tell children to write the letter that stands for the first sound in the picture name on the line. Remind children to look at the pictures in each row from left to right and to work their way through the page from top to bottom.

Grade K • Unit 2 • Week 3

Name _____

Pam at tap Sam

 _____

  _____

Phonics/Spelling
Decode Words: Say *am* and point to your mouth position. Repeat with *sat*. Write both words and model how to decode them by saying the sounds in each word and then blending them together to say each word. Then have children decode the words at the top of the page. **Spell Words:** Tell children to write the word that names the picture on the lines. Then dictate the words *mat, sat, at, am,* and *Tam* for children to spell.

Name _____

🍎   a   like   see

★   we   the   a

🌲   the   like   we

🐟   see   a   the

Review High-Frequency Words
Have children follow these directions:
🍎 Circle the word *see*.   ★ Circle the word *the*.
🌲 Circle the word *we*.   🐟 Circle the word *a*.
Dictate the words *the, we, see, a,* and *like* for children to spell.

Grade K • Unit 2 • Week 3   107

Name _____

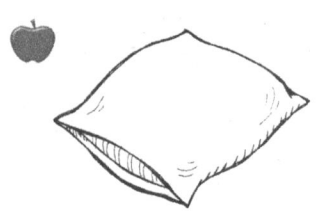

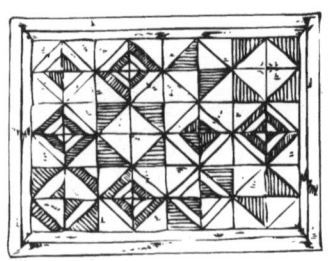

Category Words: Textures
Explain to children that things can feel different. Say: *Cotton* is soft but a *book* is hard. *Silk* is a smooth fabric. *Sandpaper* is rough.

🍎 Circle the pictures of things that are soft.
★ Circle the pictures of things that are hard.
🌲 Circle the pictures of things that are rough.
Encourage children to use texture words in sentences with a partner.

Name _____

Category Words Review
🍎 Circle the pictures in this row that show feelings.
★ Circle the pictures in this row that show shapes.
🌲 Circle the pictures in this row that show things that are yellow.
Encourage children to use feeling, shape, and color words in sentences with a partner.

Grade K • Unit 2 • Week 3   109

Name _____

🍎 We dance to the music.

⭐ The frog jumps.

🌲 He runs fast.

🐟 The boy rides the bike.

Grammar: Verbs
Remind children that a verb is a word that tells about an action. Say: *The word* eats *is a verb because it tells about an action, or what someone is doing.* The words *walks* and *hops* are verbs. Tell children to listen to each sentence and circle the verb in each one. Then have children refer back to a piece of writing that they did during the week and make sure they used verbs or action words correctly.

Name _____

🍎 The child _____.

short   writes

⭐ Pam _____.

jumps   up

🌲 The frog _____.

far   leaps

🐟 The man _____.

fishes   rod

Grammar: Verbs
Point to and name the pictures on the page. Then read each sentence and the two answer choices. Tell children to write the verb that completes each sentence on the line.

Grade K • Unit 2 • Week 3   **111**

Name _____

🍎 Can i sit?

⭐ we like to nap.

🌲 Nat Can pat the cat.

🐟 We can go?

Edit/Proofread
Tell children to listen as you read aloud the sentences. Have them rewrite each sentence so each one shows correct capitalization and end punctuation.

Name _____

We like the 🐛🦋!
bugs

Connect to Community
Encourage children to read the story to a family member or a friend.

4

Grade K · Unit 2 · Week 3

See the 🐝🦋!
bugs

We see a 🐝.
bee

Review High-Frequency Words: *the, a, see, we, like*
Have children set a purpose for reading, such as finding out what the children see. Point to the space between each word on page 1. Then encourage children to point to the space between each word on page 2.

TEKS: K.(5)(A), K.(2)(D)(iii)

1

We see a butterfly.

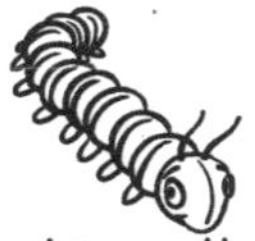

3

We see a caterpillar.

2

Name _____

  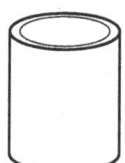 

Phonological Awareness: Recognize Rhyme
Remind children that words that rhyme have the same ending sounds. Now point to and say the names of the pictures in each row on the page. Have children circle the two pictures in each row that have names that rhyme.

Grade K • Unit 3 • Week 1   115

 Name _____

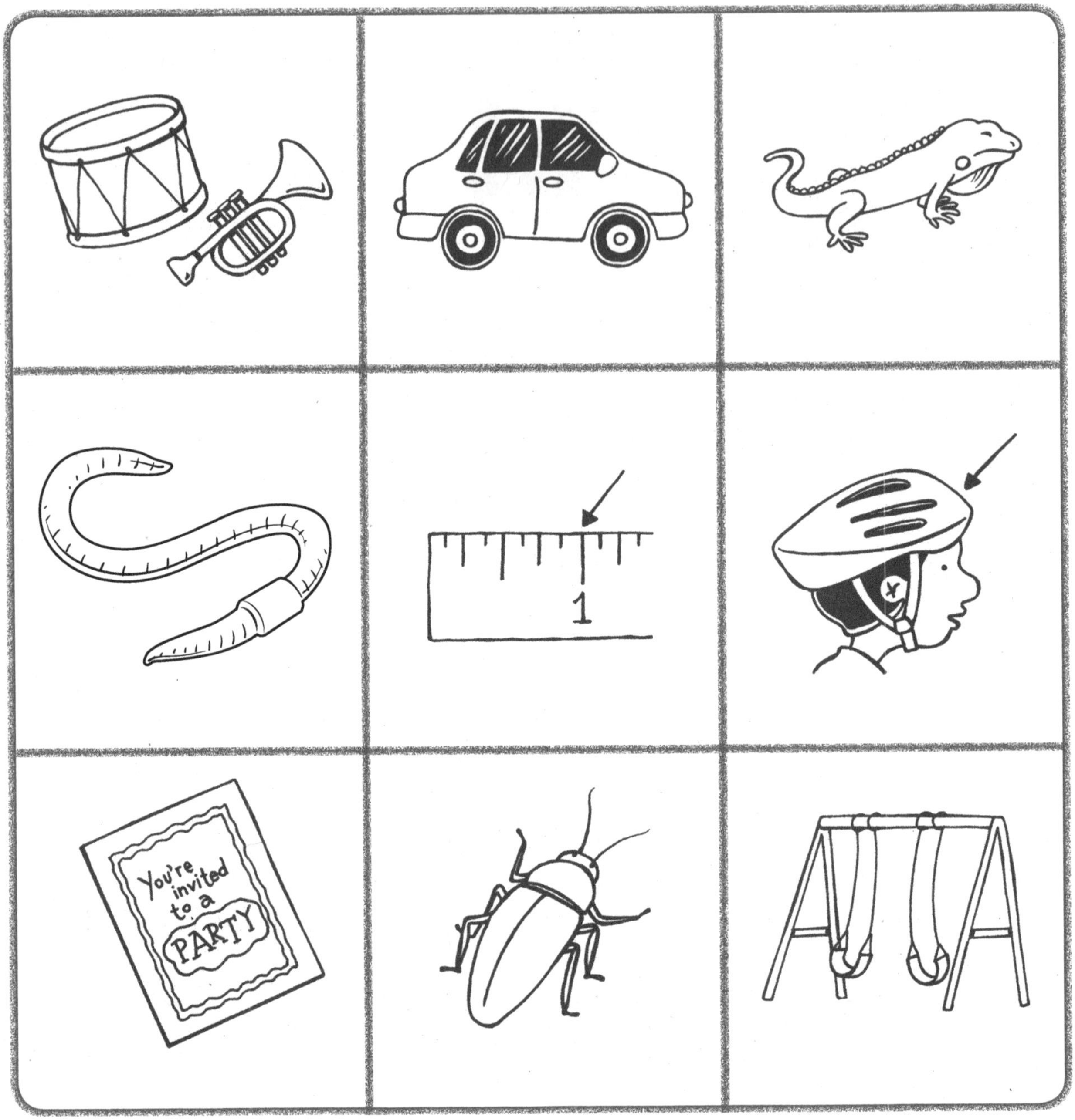

Phonemic Awareness: /i/
Point to and say the name of the picture of the instruments. Tell children that the word *instruments* begins with the /i/ sound. Have children repeat, *instruments*, /i/. Now point to and say the names of the rest of the pictures on the page. Tell children to circle the pictures that have names that begin with the /i/ sound as in *instruments*. Tell children to look at the pictures in each row from left to right and work their way down the page from top to bottom.

Name _____

Phonemic Awareness: Phoneme Blending with /i/
Tell children to listen to the sounds in the word *tip*. Model blending the sounds /t/ /i/ /p/ to say the word *tip*. Have children repeat. Then tell children you will say the sounds in more words. Have them blend the sounds to say each word. Then have them draw a picture of the word: 🍎 /p//i//n/; ⭐ /m//i//t/; 🌲 /s/ /i/ /p/; 🐟 /p/ /i/ /t/.

Grade K • Unit 3 • Week 1 117

Name _____

Phonics: /i/i
Point to the first picture and say the word *inch*. Tell children that *inch* begins with the /i/ sound. Explain that the letter *i* stands for the /i/ sound. Now point to and say the names of the rest of the pictures on the page. Have children write the letter *i* next to the picture if its name begins with the /i/ sound as in *inch*. Remind children to look at the pictures in each row from left to right and work their way from the top of the page to the bottom.

118 Grade K • Unit 3 • Week 1

Name _____

it   sat   tip   sip
_____

Phonics/Spelling
Decode Words: Say *it* and point to your mouth position. Write *it* and model how to decode it. Then have children decode the words at the top of the page. **Spell Words:** Have children point to and name each picture. Then have them spell the name of each picture and write it on the line provided: 🍎 /sssiiit/, *sit*; ⭐ /tiiimmm/, *Tim*. Then say the words *it* and *at* for children to spell.

Grade K • Unit 3 • Week 1   119

Name _____

i

m

a

t

p

Phonics: Letter/Sound Match
Point to the first letter and explain to children that this letter stands for the /i/ sound: Say the name of each picture. Point out that *insect* starts with the /i/ sound so you will draw a line from the letter *i* to the insect. Then tell children to draw a line from each letter to the picture whose name begins with that letter and sound. Have children identify the sound for each letter.

Name _____

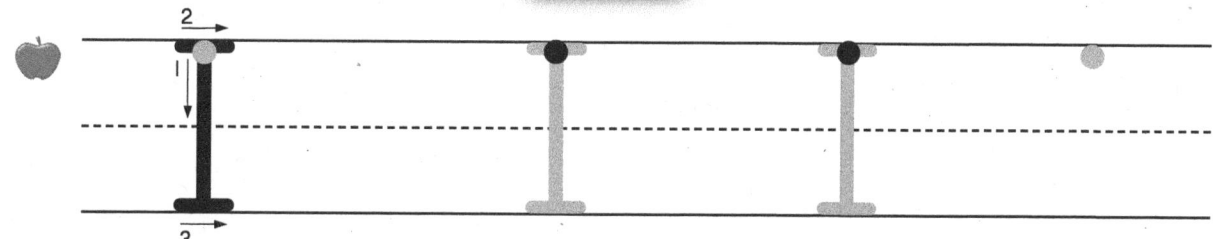

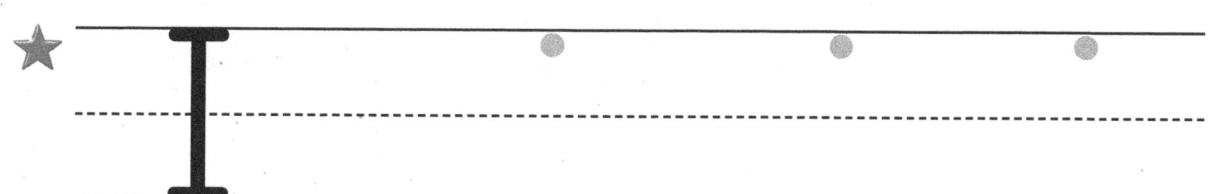

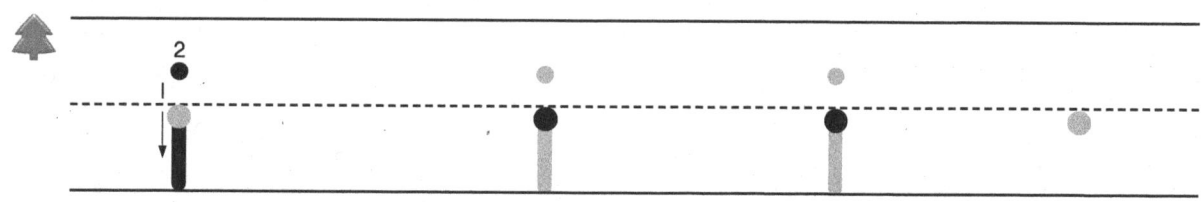

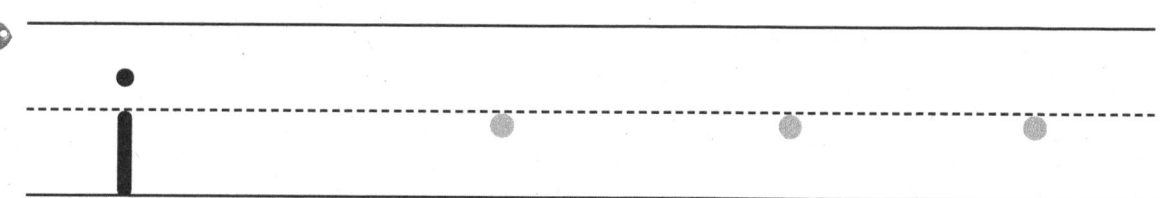

Handwriting: *Ii*
Demonstrate to children the proper formation of the uppercase and lowercase *Ii*. For the uppercase *I*, say: *Straight down. Go back to the top. Straight across. Go to the bottom line. Straight across.* For the lowercase *i* say: *Straight down, dot above.* Have children use their finger to trace the model for the letter. Then have them write the uppercase and lowercase forms of the letter *Ii*.

Grade K • Unit 3 • Week 1   **121**

Name _____

to   like

_____

🍎 I go _____ school.

_____

⭐ We _____ to run.

_____

🌲 Tam can go _____ the library.

_____

🐟 I _____ to jump.

High-Frequency Words: *to, like*
Model the Read/Spell/Write routine using the word *to*. Have children repeat the routine. Then model the Read/Spell/Write routine using the word *like*. Have children repeat using the routine. Point to and name the pictures on the page. Then tell children to write the word that completes each sentence on the lines. Model reading each sentence. Then have partners read the sentences to each other. Say aloud the words *to* and *like* for children to spell.

Name _____

Category Words: Action Words
Explain to children that people and animals can move. Say that the words *walk* and *hop* are action words. Tell children that some of the pictures on this page show someone or something moving. Point to and name the pictures in each row. Have children circle the two pictures in each row that show someone or something moving. Encourage pairs of children to use the action words in sentences.

Name _____

🍎 The puppy runs to the flowers.

★ has pretty pink flowers

🌲 Zack wrote a story.

🐟 the cute little baby

Grammar: Sentences
Explain to children that a sentence tells a complete idea. Say: *The children play* is a complete sentence. Explain that a sentence always begins with a capital letter and has an end mark, such as a period. Then say: *play in the park* is not a sentence because it does not tell a complete idea. Then read each example and point to and name the pictures. Tell children to circle the example if it is a complete sentence. Then tell them to refer back to a piece of writing they did during the week and make sure that each of their sentences tells a complete idea and has correct capitalization and end punctuation.

Name _____

🍎 I wear a seatbelt in the car.

⭐ We follow the rules of the game.

🌲 big dog barks.

🐟 The nice teacher.

Grammar: Sentences
Read each example and point to and name the pictures. Remind children that a sentence tells a complete idea. Tell children to circle the example only if it is a complete sentence. Use gestures to clarify meaning.

Grade K • Unit 3 • Week 1   125

Name _____

🍎 Can tim tap?

⭐ Sam can sit

🌲 Did Pam tap.

🐟 can we run.

Edit/Proofread
Tell children to listen as you read aloud the sentences. Have them rewrite each sentence so it shows correct capitalization and punctuation. Use gestures to clarify meaning. Tell children to refer back to a piece of writing that they did during the week and make sure they used correct capitalization and end punctuation. Tell children to also check to see that they used spelling patterns to help them spell words correctly.

Name _____

We Like to Tap

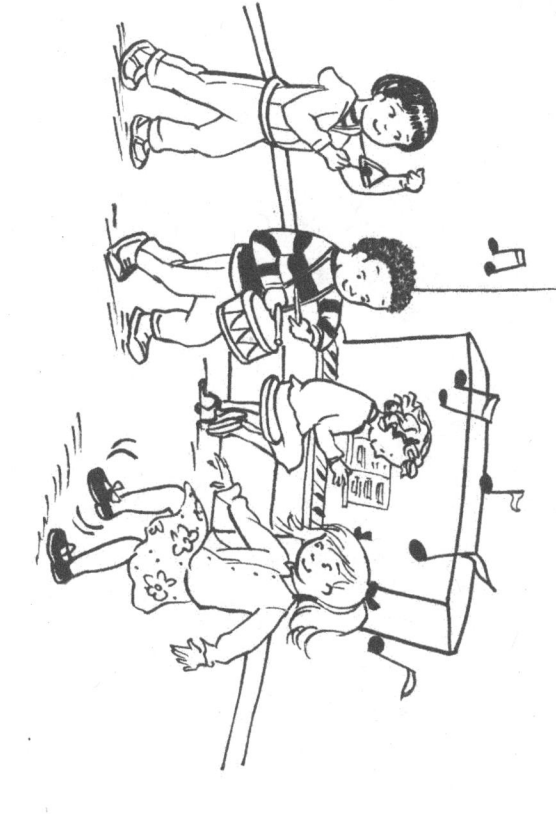

I like to tap the piano．

Review High-Frequency Words
Have children set a purpose for reading, such as finding out what instruments the children like to tap. Explain that words in a sentence are separated by spaces. Point to the space between the words *to* and *tap* on page 1. Then ask children to point to the space between the words *like* and *to* on page 4.

TEKS: K.(5)(A), K.(2)(D)(iii)

1

I like to tap to the music ！

Connect to Community
Encourage children to read the story to a family member or a friend.

Grade K · Unit 3 · Week 1

4

I like to tap the  triangle.

I like to tap the drum.

Name _____

Phonological Awareness: Onset and Rime Blending
Say the word *nap*. Then say /n//ap/, *nap*. Have children repeat. Explain that you first said the beginning sound in the word *nap* and then you said the remaining sounds. Say that you blended the sounds together to say *nap*. Tell children that you will say the beginning and ending sounds in some words. Have them blend the sounds together to say the word. Then tell children to draw a picture of the word in each box.
🍎 /n//et/, *net*; ★ /t//en/, *ten*; 🌲 /p//an/, *pan*; 🐟 /p//in/, *pin*.

Grade K • Unit 3 • Week 2   129

 Name _____

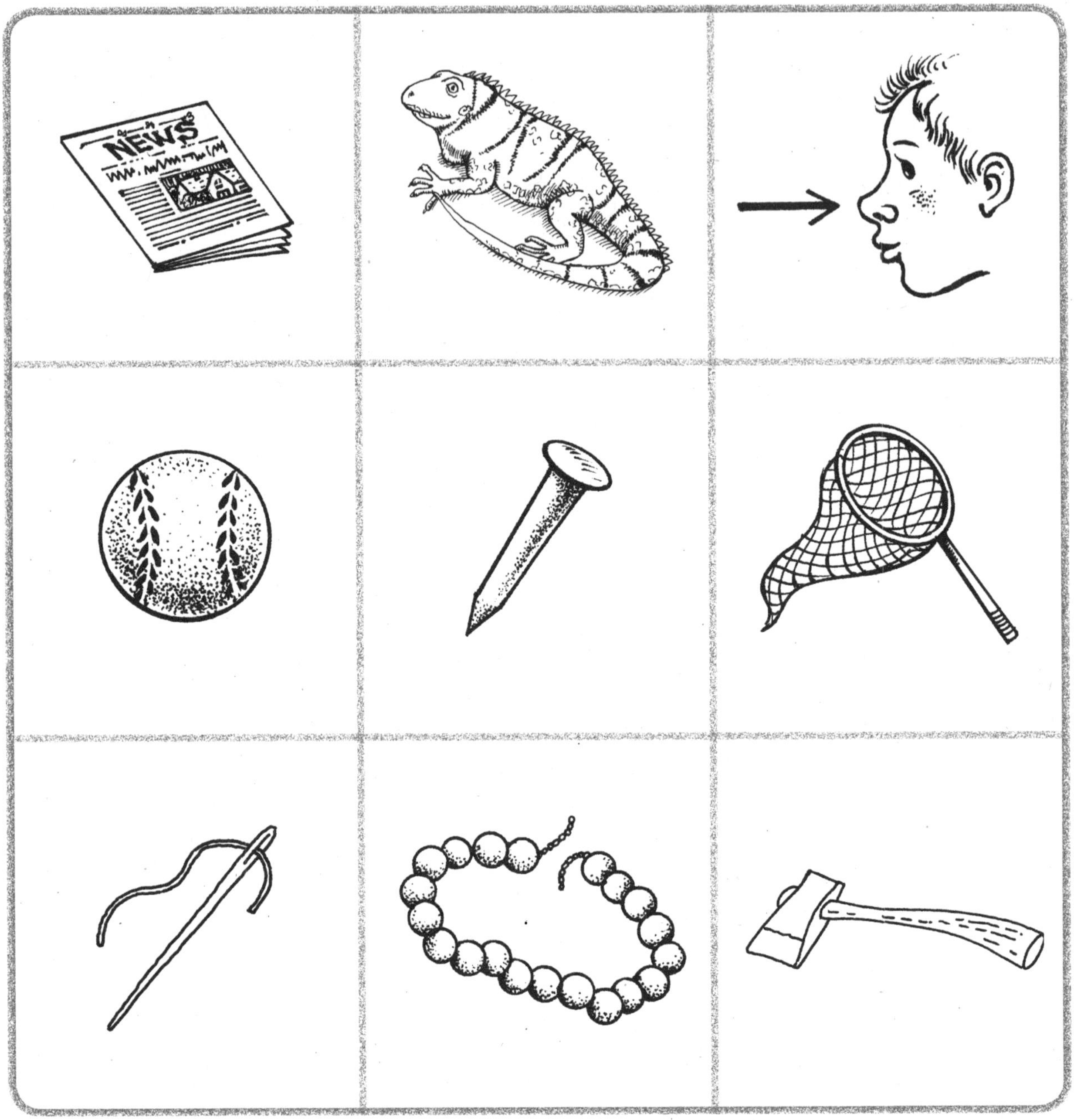

Phonemic Awareness: /n/
Point to and say the name of the picture of the newspaper. Tell children that the word *newspaper* begins with the /n/ sound. Have children repeat, *newspaper*, /n/. Now point to and say the names of the rest of the pictures on the page. Tell children to circle the pictures that have names that begin with the /n/ sound as in *newspaper*.

130 Grade K • Unit 3 • Week 2

Name _____

Phonemic Awareness: Phoneme Blending with /n/
Tell children to listen to the sounds in the word *Nat*. Model blending the sounds to say the word *Nat* /nnnaaat/, *Nat*. Have children repeat. Then tell children you will say the sounds in more words. Have them blend the sounds to say each word. Then have them draw a picture of the word: 🍎 /n//e//t/; ★ /p//e//n/; 🌲 /n//u//t/; 🐟 /p//a//n/.

Grade K • Unit 3 • Week 2 131

Phonics: /n/n
Point to and say the name of the picture of the newspaper. Tell children that the word *newspaper* begins with the /n/ sound. Explain that the letter *n* stands for the /n/ sound. Now point to and say the name of the rest of the pictures on the page. Have children write the letter *n* next to the picture if its name begins with the /n/ sound as in *newspaper*. Tell children to look at the pictures in each row from left to right. Then tell them to work their way from the top of the page to the bottom.

Grade K • Unit 3 • Week 2

Name _____

in tan it pin

_____
- - - - - - - - - - - - - - - - -
_____

_____
- - - - - - - - - - - - - - - - -
_____

_____
- - - - - - - - - - - - - - - - -
_____

Phonics/Spelling
Decode Words: Say *tin*. Point out that there are three sounds: /t/ /i/ /n/. Explain that the letters *t, i, n* stand for the sounds. Repeat with *nap*. Write both words and model how to decode them. Then have children decode the words at the top of the page. **Spell Words:** Model how to spell the words *at* and *mat* by writing a letter for each sound. Then decode the words. Say: *Some words end with the same sounds and spelling pattern, such as at and mat. Use a spelling pattern to write the picture names.*

Grade K • Unit 3 • Week 2

Name _____

n

m

i

t

p

Phonics: Letter/Sound Match
Point to the first letter and explain to children that this letter stands for the /n/ sound. Say the name of each picture. Then tell children to draw a line from each letter to the picture whose name begins with that letter.

Name _____

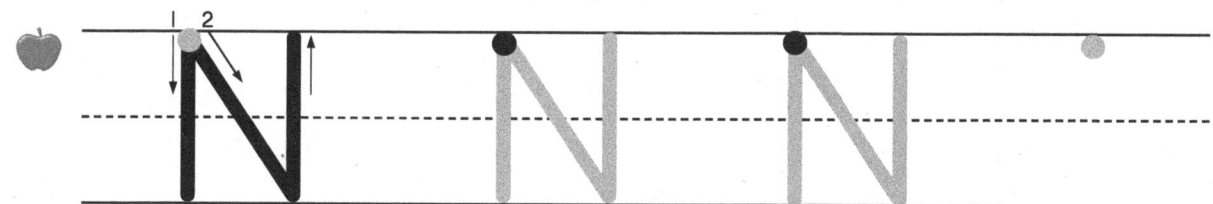

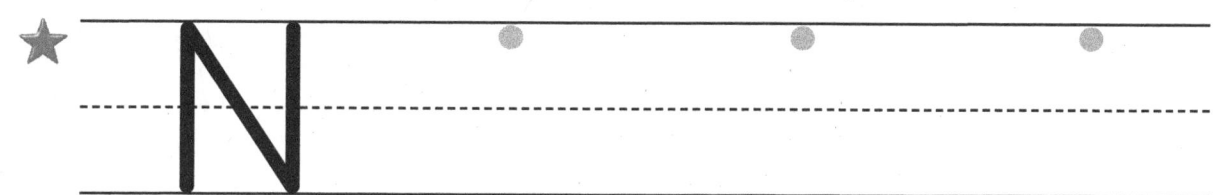

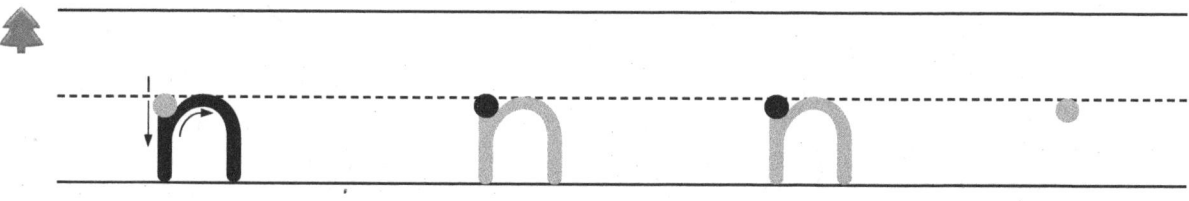

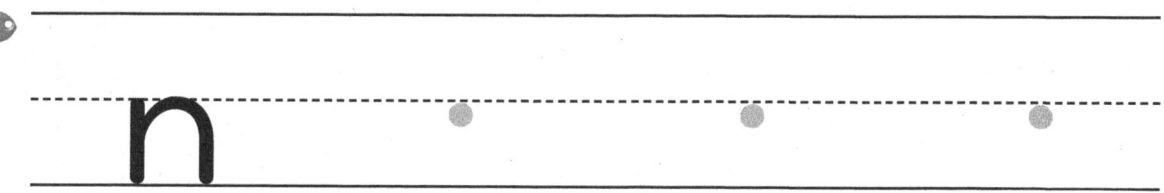

Handwriting: *Nn*
Demonstrate to children the proper formation of the uppercase and lowercase *Nn*. For the uppercase *N* say: *Straight down. Go back to the top. Slant down. Straight up.* For the lowercase *n* say: *Straight down. Around and straight down.* Have children use their finger to trace the model for the letter. Then have them write the uppercase and lowercase forms of the letter *Nn*.

Grade K • Unit 3 • Week 2

Name _____

| and   to |

_____

🍎 The boy can run _____ kick.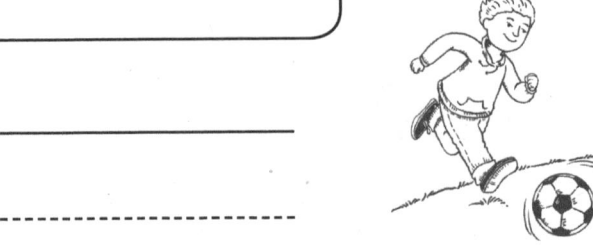

_____

⭐ We can go _____ the playground.

_____

🌲 I can read _____ write.

_____

🐟 Do you like _____ jump?

High-Frequency Words: *and, to*
Model the Read/Spell/Write routine using the word *and*. Have children repeat the routine. Remind children that the other word in the box is *to*. Tell children to repeat. Have children then write a word from the box on a line to complete each sentence. Read the sentences and have children repeat. Then say the words *and* and *to* aloud for children to spell. Tell children to make sure they spelled the words correctly.

Name _____

  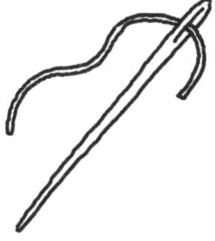

Category Words: Sound Words
Explain to children that people, animals, and things make sounds. Point to and name the pictures in each row. Have children circle the two pictures in each row that show someone or something making a sound.

Grade K • Unit 3 • Week 2   137

Name _____

🍎 hear the sounds from the sky.

★ The school band played.

🌲 In the barn.

🐟 The bird can talk.

Grammar: Sentences
Remind children that a sentence tells a complete idea. Say: *A sentence begins with a capital letter and ends with a punctuation mark, such as a period.* Read each example and point to and name the pictures. Tell children to circle the example if it is a complete sentence. Use gestures to clarify meaning.

Name _____

🍎 The dog barks.

⭐ lives in the ocean

🌲 My mom is a doctor.

🐟 can beep

Grammar: Sentences
Remind children that a sentence tells a complete idea. It usually contains a noun and a verb. Say: *For example, some sentences tell a fact about someone or something and have a period at the end.* Read each example. Tell children to circle each example that is a complete sentence. Remind children also that a sentence begins with an uppercase letter and has end punctuation. Then have children refer back to a piece of writing they did during the week and make sure they used complete sentences and correct capitalization and that they added a period at the end of sentences that tell facts.

Name _____

🍎 Nat and Pam s i t.

⭐ Nan cansee a man.

🌲 We like the can and the pan

🐟 can you nap on the mat.

Edit/Proofread
Tell children to listen as you read aloud the sentences. Have them rewrite each sentence so it shows correct capitalization and punctuation. Use gestures to clarify meaning. Tell children to refer back to a piece of writing that they did during the week and make sure they used correct capitalization and end punctuation.

Name _____

The Map

Sam and Pam draw .

Review High-Frequency Words
Have children set a purpose for reading, such as finding out what the children do with the map. Explain that words are made up of letters. Model by pointing to the word *and* on page 1 and then to the letter *a* in the word. Then ask children to point to a word on page 4 and then to a letter in the word.

TEKS: K.(2)(D)(iv), K.(5)(A)

Sam and Pam see it.

Connect to Community
Encourage children to read the story to a family member or a friend.

Grade K • Unit 3 • Week 2

Sam and Pam  run.

Sam and Pam  read it.

Name _____

Phonological Awareness: Count and Pronounce Syllables
Point to the table and say its name. Model clapping for each syllable in the word. Point out that there are two parts or syllables in *table*. Tell children that you will write the number 2 in the box because *table* has two parts or syllables. Point to and name the remaining pictures. Tell children to say the parts in each word and write a number in the box to show how many parts or syllables they hear.

Grade K • Unit 3 • Week 3 143

 Name _____

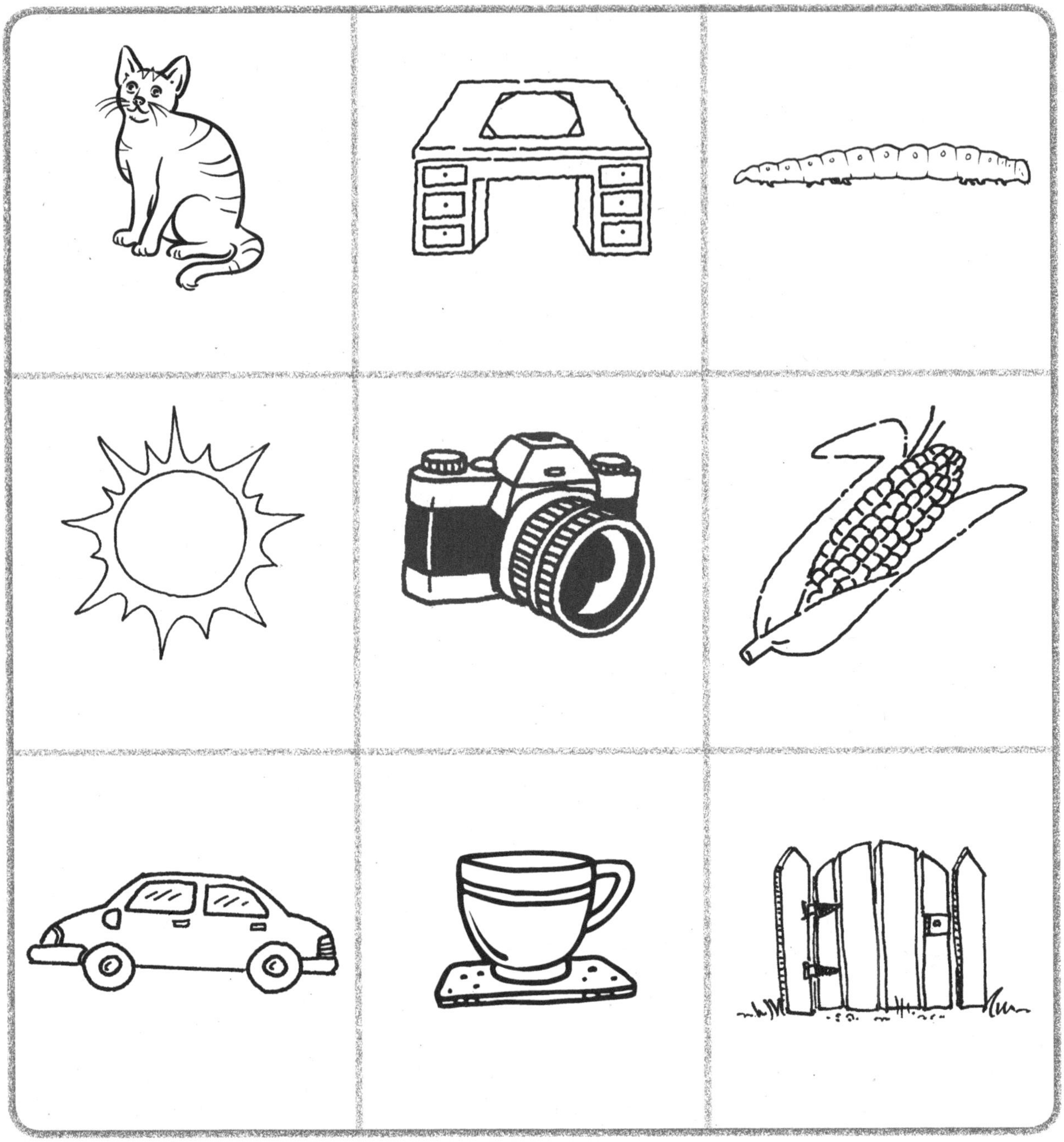

Phonemic Awareness: /k/c
Point to and say the name of the picture of the cat. Tell children that the word *cat* begins with the /k/ sound. Have children repeat, *cat*, /k/. Now point to and say the names of the rest of the pictures on the page. Tell children to circle the pictures that have names that begin with the /k/ sound as in *cat*. Tell children to look at the pictures in each row from left to right and work their way down the page from top to bottom.

Name _____

Phonemic Awareness: /k/c
Point to and say the name of the pictures on the page. Tell children to circle the pictures that have names that begin with the /k/ sound as in *cut*. Tell children to look at the pictures in each row from left to right and work their way down the page from top to bottom.

Phonics: /k/c

Point to and say the name of the picture of the comb. Tell children that the word *comb* begins with the /k/ sound. Explain that the letter *c* stands for the /k/ sound. Now point to and say the name of the rest of the pictures on the page. Have children write the letter *c* next to the picture if its name begins with /k/ sound as in *comb*. Tell children to look at the pictures in each row from left to right. Then tell them to work their way from the top of the page to the bottom.

146 Grade K • Unit 3 • Week 3

Name _____

can   tap   Cam   pin

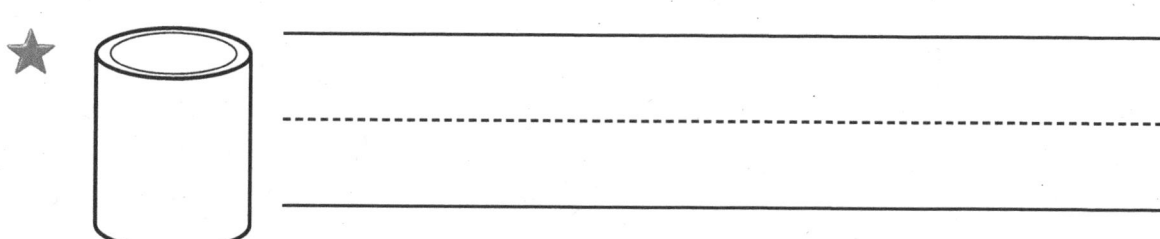

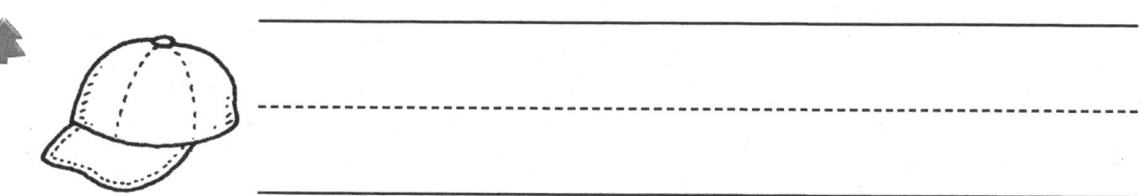

Phonics/Spelling
Decode Words: Say *Cam* and point to your mouth position. Write the word and model how to decode it as you say each sound in the name and then blend the sounds together to say *Cam*. Then have children decode the words at the top of the page. **Spell Words:** Have children write the word that names each picture.

Grade K • Unit 3 • Week 3   **147**

Name _____

c

s

p

t

i

Phonics
Point to the first letter and explain to children that this letter stands for the /k/ sound. Say the name of each picture. Then tell children to draw a line from each letter to the picture whose name begins with that letter.

Name _____

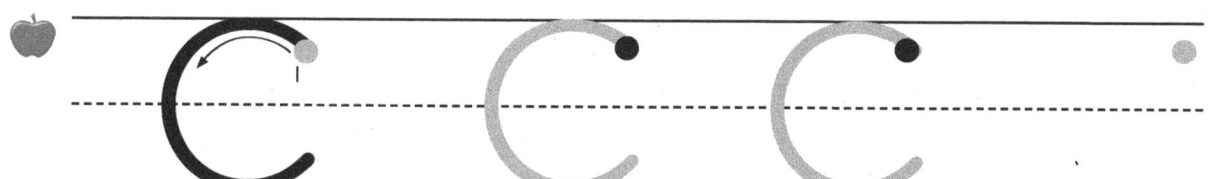

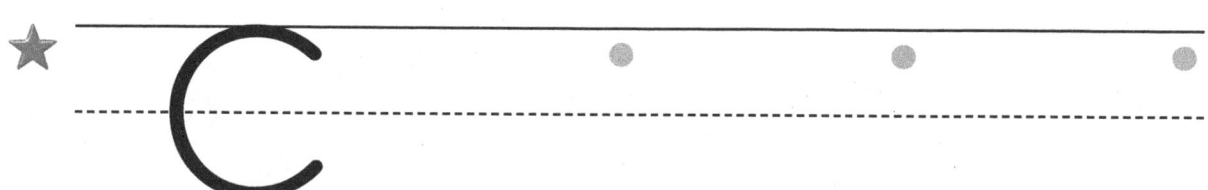

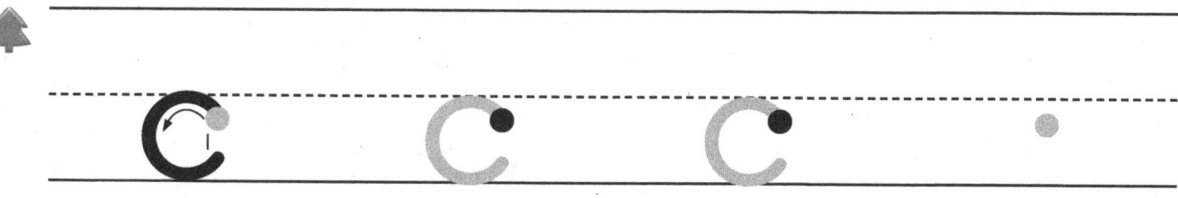

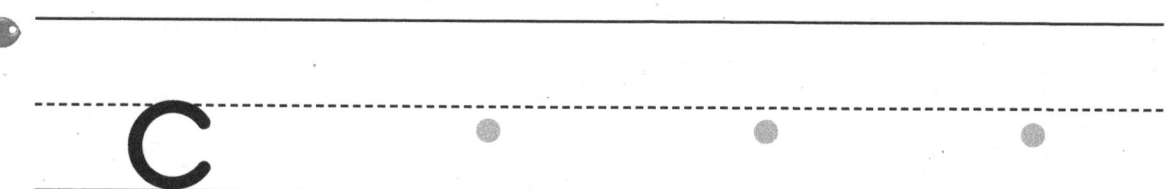

Handwriting: *Cc*
Demonstrate to children the proper formation of the uppercase and lowercase *Cc*. For the uppercase *C* say: *Circle back and around, then stop.* For the lowercase *c* say: *Circle back and around, then stop.* Have children use their finger to trace the model for the letter. Then have them write the uppercase and lowercase forms of the letter *Cc*.

Grade K • Unit 3 • Week 3

Name _____

| go   and |

_____
- - - - - - -

🍎 I can _____ to school.

_____
- - - - - - -

⭐ You _____ I like to read.

_____
- - - - - - -

🌲 The girl can _____ on the swing.

_____
- - - - - - -

🐟 Go with Tim _____ Cam.

High-Frequency Words: *go, and*
Model the Read/Spell/Write routine using the word *go*. Have children repeat the routine using the words *go* and *and*. Then have children write a word from the box on a line to complete each sentence. Read the sentences and have children repeat. Then say the words *go* and *and* aloud for children to spell. Tell children to make sure they spelled the words correctly.

Name _____

Category Words: Sequence Words
Explain that things happen in a certain order. Tell children that on a school day, for example, they first wake up, then get dressed, and finally they eat breakfast before going to school. Explain that the pictures on this page show the steps in making apple cake to sell at a market. Point to and describe each picture. Have children look at the pictures and write a number for what happens *first, next,* and *last.* Encourage partners to use these words as they talk about the order of the pictures.

Name _____

🍎 Where is the library?

★ reads many books there.

🌲 What is your favorite book?

🐟 plays soccer?

Grammar: Sentences
Remind children that a sentence tells a complete idea. A sentence begins with a capital letter and ends with a punctuation mark, such as a period, a question mark, or an exclamation mark. Then read each example and point to and name the pictures. Tell children to circle the example if it is a complete sentence. Then tell children to refer to a piece of writing that they did during the week and make sure they used correct capitalization and end punctuation. Tell children to also use spelling patterns to help them write words as well as use the correct spelling of high-frequency words.

Name _____

_____ lives at the zoo?

Who   When

_____ is the zoo?

When   Where

_____ does the play start?

Who   When

Grammar: Sentences
Explain that some sentences ask questions. Some question words are *Who, When, Where, How*. Then read the sentences and word choices. Point to and say the name of each picture. Then tell children to write the word that completes each sentence on the lines. Use gestures to clarify meaning. Tell children to refer back to a piece of writing that they did during the week and make sure they used question marks in their sentences correctly.

Grade K • Unit 3 • Week 3   153

Name _____

🍎 Can Nan see the cat.

⭐ The cat can nap on the Mat.

🌲 Can Tim see the cap.

🐟 Go with me?

Edit/Proofread
Tell children to listen as you read aloud the sentences. Have them rewrite each sentence so it shows correct capitalization and punctuation. Remind children that a sentence begins with an uppercase letter and ends with an end punctuation mark, such as a period or question mark. Say that a sentence tells a complete idea. Use gestures to clarify meaning.

Name _____

We go home.

Connect to Community
Encourage children to read the story to a family member or a friend.

Grade K · Unit 3 · Week 3

4

We go to the store.

Review High-Frequency Words
Have children set a purpose for reading, such as finding out where the bears go. Then tell children that they read from left to right. Model this concept of directionality for children.

TEKS: K.5(A), K.(2)(D)(ii)

1

We go to the 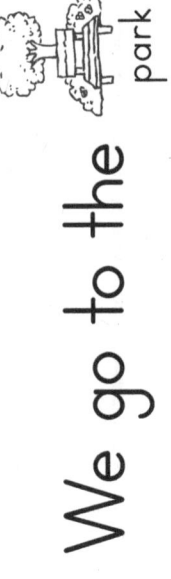 park.

We go to the  bakery.

Name _____

Phonological Awareness: Onset and Rime Segmentation
Explain to children that words are made up of beginning and ending sounds. Say the word *sit*. Tell children that the beginning sound is /s/. Then say that the ending sounds are /iiit/, *it*. Tell children to say the word, *sit*. Tell children that you will draw a picture of a person sitting in the first box. Then say some words and encourage children to say the beginning and ending sounds in each word. Have children draw a picture in each box that shows the word. ★ *sad, /s//ad/;* 🌲 *mat, /m//at/;* 🐟 *sun, /s//un/.*

Grade K • Unit 4 • Week 1 157

 Name _____

Phonemic Awareness: /o/ o
Point to and say the name of the picture of the olive. Tell children that the word *olive* begins with the /o/ sound. Have children repeat, *olive*, /o/. Now point to and say the names of the rest of the pictures on the page. Tell children to circle the pictures that have names that begin with the /o/ sound as in *olive*. Tell children to look at the pictures in each row from left to right and work their way down the page from top to bottom.

158   Grade K • Unit 4 • Week 1

Name _____

1.	2.
3.	4.

Phonemic Awareness: Phoneme Blending with /o/
Tell children to listen to the sounds in the word *on*. Model blending the sounds to say the word *on*, /ooonnn/, *on*. Have children repeat. Tell children you will say the sounds in more words. Have them blend the sounds to say each word. Then have them draw a picture of the following words in the correct box:
1. /p//o//t/; 2. /d//o//t/; 3. /b/ /o/ /ks/; 4. /m//o//p/.

Grade K • Unit 4 • Week 1   159

Name _____

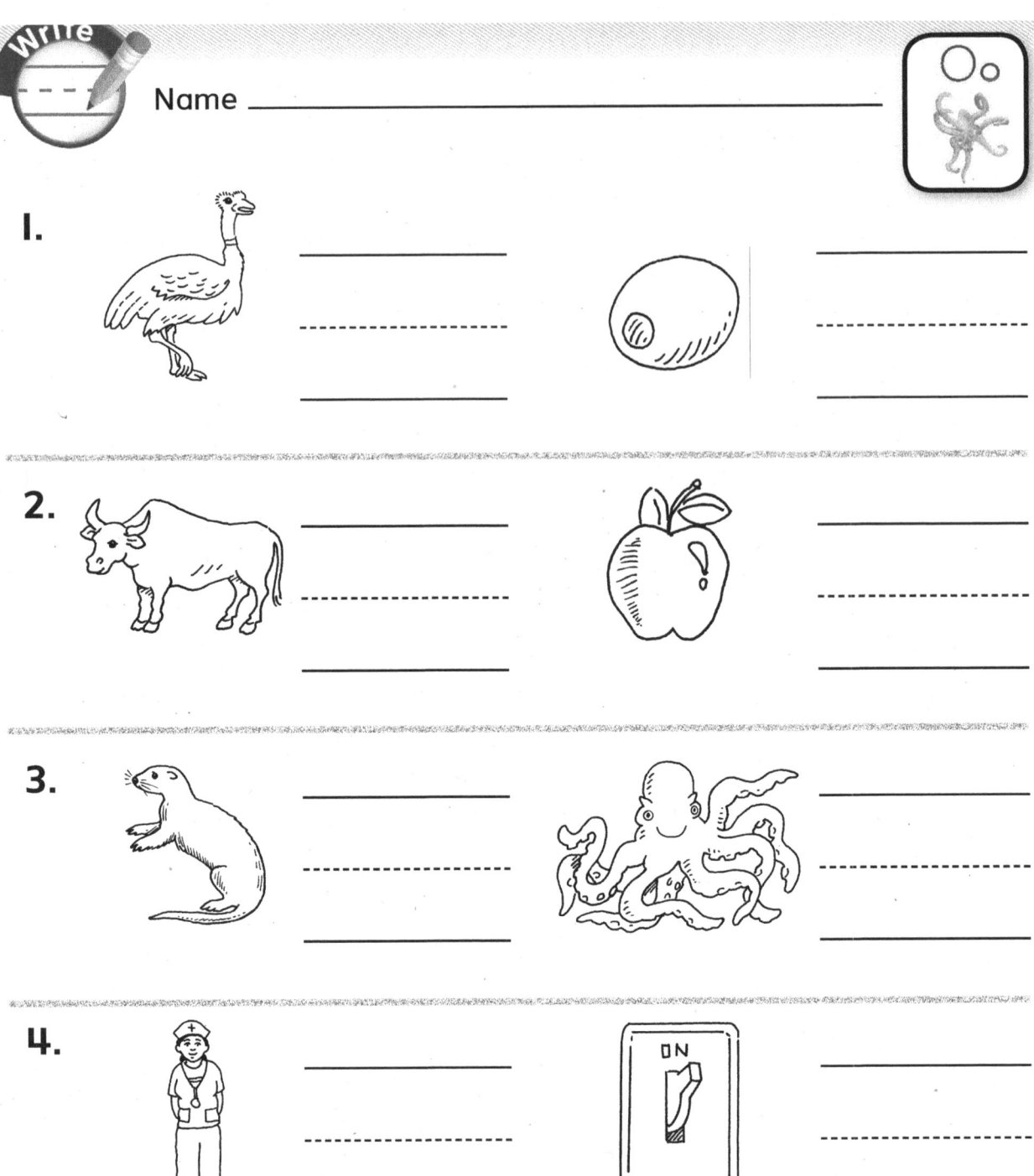

Phonics: /o/o
Point to and say the word *ostrich* in the first row. Tell children that *ostrich* begins with the /o/ sound. Explain that the letter *o* stands for the /o/ sound. Now point to and say the names of the rest of the pictures on the page. Have children write the letter *o* next to the picture if its name begins with the /o/ sound as in *ostrich*. Remind children to look at the pictures in each row from left to right and work their way from the top of the page to the bottom.

160 Grade K • Unit 4 • Week 1

Name _____

on pop can cot

1.

2.

3.

Phonics/Spelling
Decode Words: Say *not* and point to your mouth position. Write *not* and model how to decode it by saying each sound and then blending the sounds together to say *not*. Repeat with *in* and *on*. Then have children decode the words at the top of the page. **Spell Words:** Have children write the word that names each picture.

 Name _____

o

a

c

n

i

Phonics: Letter/Sound Match
Point to the letter *o* and explain to children that this letter stands for the /o/ sound. Say the name of each picture. Then tell children to draw a line from each letter to the picture whose name begins with that letter and sound.

162   Grade K • Unit 4 • Week 1

Name _____

1.

2.

3.

4.

Handwriting: *Oo*
Demonstrate to children the proper formation of the uppercase and lowercase *Oo*. For the uppercase *O* say: *Circle back, then around all the way.* For the lowercase *o*, repeat: *Circle back, then around all the way.* Have children use their finger to trace the model for the letter. Then have them write the uppercase and lowercase forms of the letter *Oo*.

Grade K • Unit 4 • Week 1 **163**

Name _____

| you   go |

1. _____ can plant the seeds.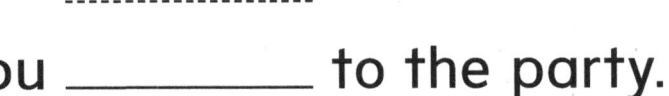

2. You _____ to the party.

3. _____ can swim.

4. _____ can cook.

High-Frequency Words: *you, go*
Model the Read/Spell/Write routine using the word *you*. Have children repeat the routine. Remind children that the other word in the box is *go*. Tell children to repeat. Have children then write a word from the box on the line to complete each sentence. Have partners read the sentences to each other. Then say the words *you* and *go* for children to spell.

Name _____

1.

2.

3.

Category Words: Job Words
Explain to children that people can do different kinds of jobs. Tell them that you are a teacher which is a kind of job. Point to and name the pictures in each row. Have children look at the pictures in each row and circle the two pictures that show people doing jobs.

Grade K • Unit 4 • Week 1   **165**

Name _____

1. We go to a big school.

2. I see a tiny mouse.

3. He ate a juicy orange.

4. The little baby crawls to me.

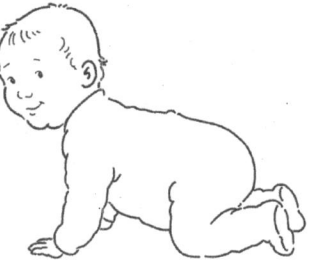

Grammar: Adjectives
Explain to children that an adjective describes something or someone. Tell them that the word *funny* describes the book when you say *The funny book makes me laugh.* Then read each sentence and point to and name the picture next to it. Tell children to circle the adjective in each sentence.

Name _____

big hot tall blue

_____
----

1. I see the _____ clouds.

_____
----

2. I sit under a _____ tree.

_____
----

3. The _____ sun shines on me.

_____
----

4. Did you see the _____ crayon?

Grammar: Adjectives
Remind children that an adjective describes something or someone. Say: *Listen to this sentence*: The funny book made me laugh! *The word* funny *is an adjective*. It describes the book. Read the sentences and point to and name the pictures. Tell children to write a word from the box to complete each sentence. Tell children to refer back to a piece of writing that they did during the week and make sure they used adjectives correctly.

Name _____

1. I can see Mom

2. Can Sam go to the top.

3. You can tap

4. Tim and Nat can play?

Edit/Proofread
Tell children to listen as you read aloud the sentences. Have them rewrite each sentence so it shows correct capitalization and punctuation. Use gestures to clarify meaning. Then have children refer to a piece of writing that they did during the week and make sure they used correct capitalization and end punctuation.

Name _____

You and I

You and I can rake.

Review High-Frequency Words
Have children set a purpose for reading, such as finding out what the children do in the garden. Point to the letter o in the word you on page 1. Tell children that words are made up of letters. Say that the letter o is a letter in the word you. Then ask children to point to the letter a in the word can on page 4.

TEKS:K.(5)(A), K.(2)(D)(iv)

1

You and I can pull.

Connect to Community
Encourage children to read the story to a family member or a friend.

4 Grade K · Unit 4 · Week 1

You and I can  water.

You and I can dig.

Name _____

1.			
2.			
3.			
4.			

Phonological Awareness: Sentence Segmentation
Remind children that sentences are made up of words. Say: *I like my neighborhood.* Tell children that there are four words in the sentence. Hold up a finger for each word in the sentence. Tell children you will color in four boxes to show that there are four words in the sentence. Then tell children to color in a box for each word that they hear in the following sentences: 2. *I have friendly neighbors.* 3. *The store opened.* 4. *Buy it!* .

 Name _____

Phonemic Awareness: /d/
Point to and say the name of the picture of the desk. Tell children that the word *desk* begins with the /d/ sound. Have children repeat, *desk*, /d/. Now point to and say the names of the rest of the pictures on the page. Tell children to circle the pictures that have names that begin with the /d/ sound as in *desk*. Tell children to look at the pictures in each row from left to right and work their way down the page from top to bottom.

172   Grade K • Unit 4 • Week 2

Name _____

1.			
2.			
3.			
4.			

Phoneme Segmentation
Tell children to listen as you say the word *dot*. Say each sound in the word *dot*, /d//o//t/. Blend the sounds together to say the word /dooot/, *dot*. Explain that there are three sounds in the word. Now say the name of each picture. Then tell children to say the sounds in each picture's name. Encourage them to then count the number of sounds they hear and color in a box for each sound.

Name _____

Phonics: /d/d
Point to and say the name of the first picture in row 1: *duck*. Say: Duck *begins with the /d/ sound*. Explain that the letter *d* stands for the /d/ sound. Now point to and say the names of the rest of the pictures on the page. Have children write the letter *d* next to the picture if its name begins with the /d/ sound as in *duck*. Remind children to look at the pictures in each row from left to right and work their way from the top of the page to the bottom.

174 Grade K • Unit 4 • Week 2

Name _____

Dad dip dim did

1.

2.

3.

Phonics/Spelling
Decode Words: Say *Dan* and point to your mouth position. Write *Dan* and model how to decode it by saying each sound in the name and then blending the sounds together to say: /D/ /a/ /n/, /Daaannn/, *Dan*. Then have children decode the words at the top of the page. **Spell Words:** Have children write the word that names each picture.

Grade K • Unit 4 • Week 2 **175**

Name _____

d

p

c

i

n

Phonics: Letter/Sound Match
Point to the first letter and explain to children that this letter stands for the /d/ sound. Say the name of each picture. Then tell children to draw a line from each letter to the picture whose name begins with that letter. Explain that you will draw a line from the letter *d* to the picture of a dad reading a book because *dad* begins with the /d/ sound spelled *d*.

Name _____

1.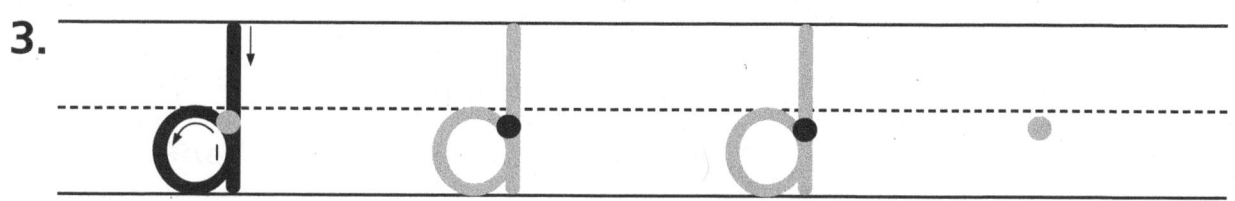

2. D

3.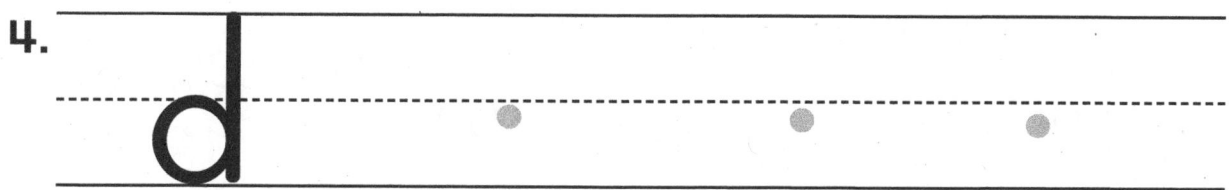

4. d

Handwriting *Dd*
Demonstrate to children the proper formation of the uppercase and lowercase letter *Dd*. Say: For the uppercase D, say: *Straight down. Go back to the top. Around and in at the bottom.* For the lowercase d, say: *Circle back and around. Go to the top line. Straight down.* Have children use their finger to trace the model for the letter. Then have them write the uppercase and lowercase forms of the letter *Dd*.

Grade K • Unit 4 • Week 2

Name _____

| do | you |

_____

1. I can _____ the laundry.

_____

2. _____ and I can dance.

_____

3. _____ you like to fish?

_____

4. I can _____ the dishes.

High-Frequency Words: *do, you*
Model the Read/Spell/Write routine using the word *do*. Have children repeat the routine. Remind children that the other word in the box is *you*. Tell children to repeat. Have children then write a word from the box on the line to complete each sentence. Have partners read the sentences to each other. Then say the words *do* and *you* for children to spell.

Name _____

1.

2.

3.

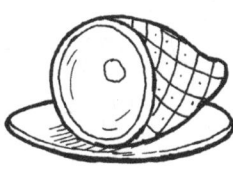  

Category Words: Kinds of Foods
Explain to children that there are different kinds of foods. Tell them that an orange, for example, is a type of fruit; string beans are a type of vegetable; a hamburger is a type of meat. Point to and name the pictures in each row. Then have children follow these directions.
1. Circle pictures of vegetables.
2. Circle pictures of fruits.
3. Circle pictures of meats.

Grade K • Unit 4 • Week 2

 Name _____

big soft tiny sweet

1. We see the _____ jet.

2. Jack sees a _____ ant.

3. My kitten has _____ fur.

4. I like the _____ orange.

Grammar: Adjectives
Remind children that a adjective describes something or someone. Read the sentences and point to and name the pictures. Tell children to write a word from the box on the lines to complete each sentence.

Name _____

1. My cat climbs the tall tree.

2. Nan eats a yellow banana.

3. Dan will wash the dirty pan.

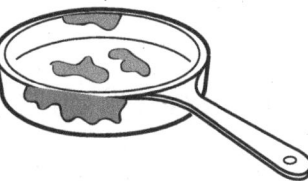

4. Mom has a soft pillow.

Grammar: Adjectives
Remind children that a adjective describes something or someone. Read the sentences and point to and name the pictures. Tell children to circle a word in each sentence that is an adjective. Then ask children to refer back to a piece of writing they did during the week and make sure they used adjectives correctly.

Grade K • Unit 4 • Week 2

Name _____

1. Do you see Tim.

2. Ican see the dot.

3. Don can d i p the pan.

4. Did Pam See Dan.

Edit/Proofread
Tell children to listen as you read aloud the sentences. Have them rewrite each sentence so it shows correct capitalization, punctuation, and spacing between words. Use gestures to clarify meaning.

Name _____

Do You?

Do you like  salad ?

I do!

Review High-Frequency Words
Have children set a purpose for reading, such as finding out what the bears like to eat. Model pointing from left to right as you read the first sentence of the story. Then ask children to point from left to right as they read the remaining sentences in the story.

Connect to Community
Encourage children to read the story to a family member or a friend.

1

4

Grade K • Unit 4 • Week 2

TEKS: K.(5)(A), K.(2)(D)(ii)

Do you like ?
pizza

3

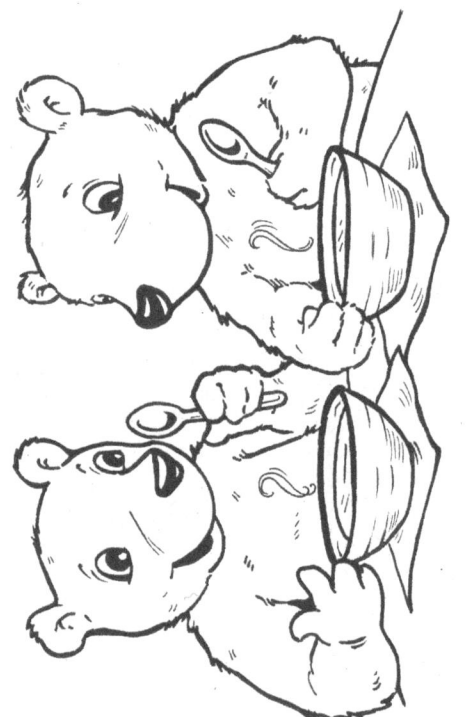

Do you like ?
soup

2

Name _____

Phonological Awareness: Recognize Rhyme
Remind children that words that rhyme have the same ending sounds. Now point to and say the names of the pictures in each row on the page. Have children circle the two pictures in each row that have names that rhyme.

Grade K • Unit 4 • Week 3

Name _____

1.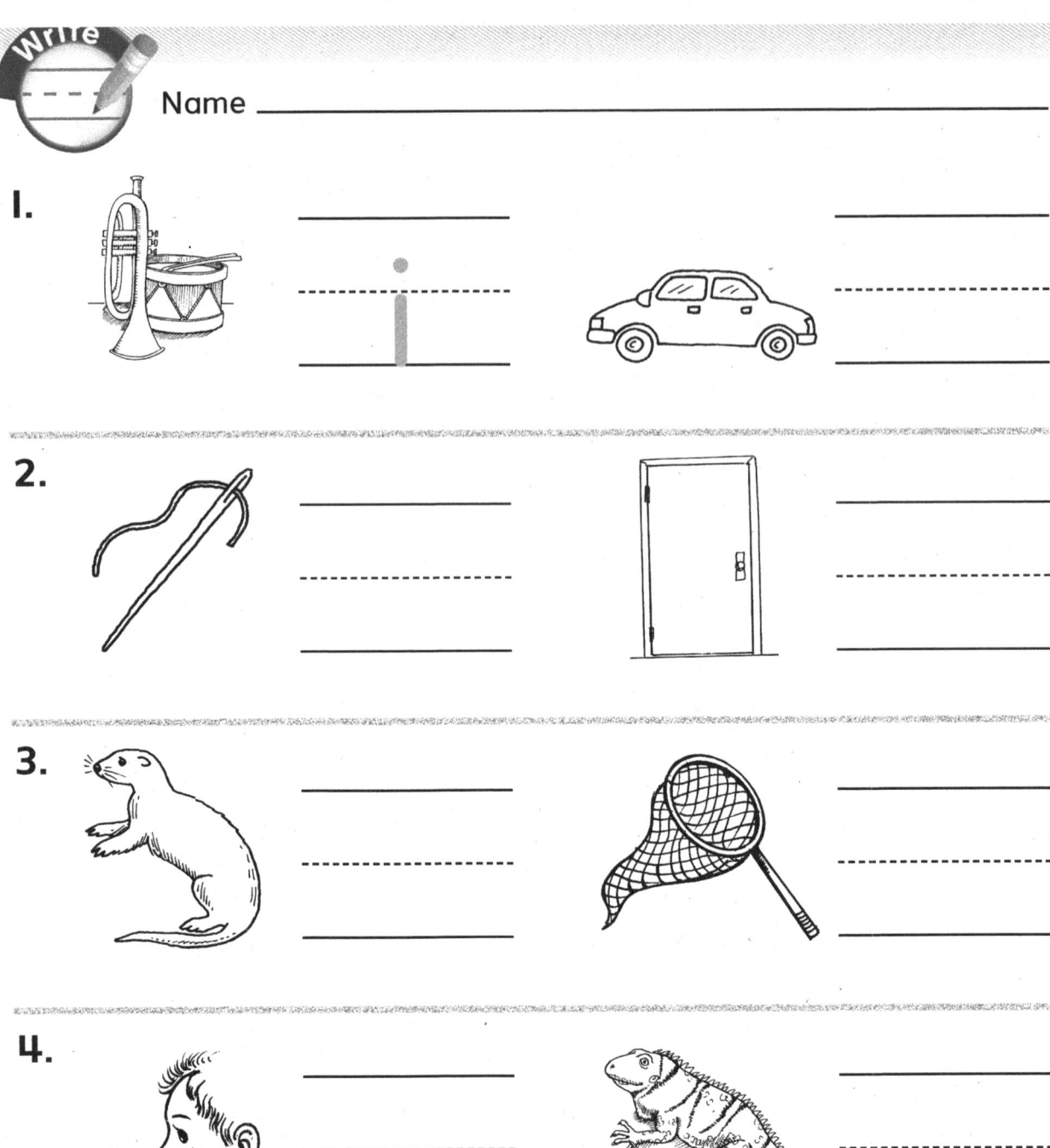

Review Phonics: /i/i, /n/n, /k/c, /o/o, /d/d
Point to the first picture in row 1 and say the word *instruments*. Tell children that *instruments* begins with the /i/ sound. Explain that the letter *i* stands for the /i/ sound. Now point to and say the names of the rest of the pictures on the page. Have children write the letter that stands for the first sound in the picture name on the lines. Remind children to look at the pictures in each row from left to right and work their way from the top of the page to the bottom.

186 Grade K • Unit 4 • Week 3

Name _____

1.    sn

2. 

3. 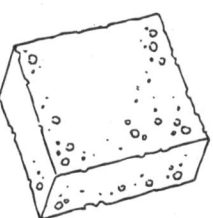

4.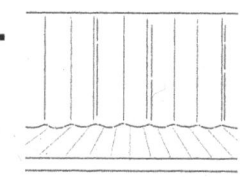

Phonics: *s*-Blends *sn, sp, st*

Point to and say the name of the first picture in row 1 and say its name: *snake*. Say: *Snake* begins with the sounds /sn/. Point out that the letters *s* and *n* together form the blend *sn*. Now point to and say the names of the rest of the pictures on the page. Have children write the blend *sn, sp,* or *st* for the beginning sounds of each picture name. Remind children to look at the pictures in each row from left to right and work their way from the top of the page to the bottom.

Grade K • Unit 4 • Week 3   **187**

Name _____

snap stop spin spot

1.

2.

3.

Phonics/Spelling
Decode Words: Say *spin*. Write the word and model how to decode it by saying and blending the sounds. Then have children decode the words at the top of the page. **Spell Words:** Model how to spell *man* and *Stan* by writing a letter for each sound. Then decode the words. Point out to children that they can identify and spell words using the sound-spelling pattern, such as words ending with /an/ as in *man* and *Stan*. Have children write the three picture names using a spelling pattern. Tell children to refer back to a piece of writing and check spelling by using spelling patterns to help them.

188 Grade K • Unit 4 • Week 3

Name _____

1. and   go   to

2. do   you   and

3. go   to   do

4. and   you   do

Review High-Frequency Words
Have children follow these directions:

1. Circle the word *go*.
2. Circle the word *you*.
3. Circle the word *to*.
4. Circle the word *do*.

Then say the words *and, do, go, to, you* for children to spell.

Grade K • Unit 4 • Week 3

Name _____

1.

2.

3.

Category Words: Position Words
Explain to children that the words *up, down, under, over, first,* and *last* tell about positions or where people or things are. Model by saying: *The paper is under my desk.* Point to and name the pictures in each row. Then have children circle the pictures that show people or animals in a certain position.

190 Grade K • Unit 4 • Week 3

Name _____

1.

2.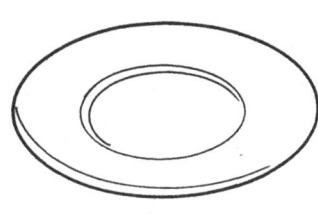

3.

Category Words Review
1. Circle the pictures in this row that show people or animals moving.
2. Circle the pictures in this row that show positions.
3. Circle the pictures in this row that show something happening first and next.

Grade K • Unit 4 • Week 3

Name _____

| fast pretty round small |

_____
----

1. The _____ mouse eats cheese.

_____
----

2. Mom looks at her _____ flowers.

_____
----

3. The bus has _____ wheels.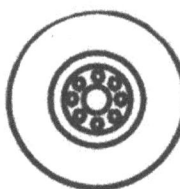

_____
----

4. The _____ train is fun.

Grammar: Adjectives
Remind children that an adjective is a word that describes someone or something. Say: The slow turtle walks by. *The word* slow *describes the turtle.* Point to and say the adjectives in the box. Read the sentences and point to and name the pictures. Help children choose a word from the box to complete each sentence. Have children refer back to a piece of writing and make sure they used adjectives correctly.

Name _____

1. The round ball is here.

2. I have curly hair.

3. The blue car drives by.

4. The happy baby smiled.

Grammar: Adjectives
Read each sentence and point to and name the pictures. Tell children to draw a line under the word in each sentence that is an adjective. Then tell children to refer back to a piece of writing that they did during the week and make sure they used adjectives correctly.

Name _____

1. Tom can sit on themat.

2. Nan can t a p the top of the pot.

3. Sid can sit on the pad

4. i sat at the top.

Edit/Proofread
Tell children to listen as you read aloud the sentences. Have them rewrite each sentence so it shows correct capitalization, punctuation, and spacing between words. Use gestures to clarify meaning. Then tell children to refer back to a piece of writing that they did during the week and make sure they used correct capitalization, end punctuation, and spacing between words.

Name _____

You and I

We can go to the park!

Review High-Frequency Words
Have children set a purpose for reading, such as finding out what the children do at the park. Explain that words in a sentence are separated by spaces. Point to the space between the words *go* and *to* on page 1. Then ask children to point to the space between the words *can* and *do* on page 4. Tell children to read from left to right.

TEKS: K.5(A), K.(2)(D)(iii), K.(2)(D)(iii)

1

You and I can do it!

Connect to Community
Encourage children to read the story to a family member or a friend.

4

Grade K • Unit 4 • Week 3

Copyright © McGraw-Hill Education

Can we do it?

We can do a 🧩 puzzle.

Back Matter

Name _____

The Alphabet

Aa 	Bb 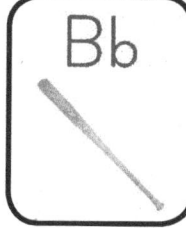	Cc 	Dd 	Ee 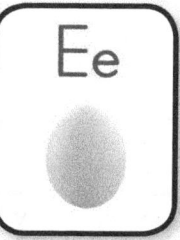	Ff 
Gg 	Hh 	Ii 	Jj 	Kk 	Ll 
Mm 	Nn 	Oo 	Pp 	Qq 	Rr 
Ss 	Tt 	Uu 	Vv 	Ww 	Xx 
Yy 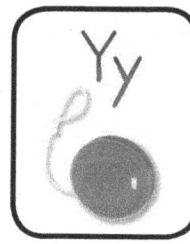	Zz 				

Handwriting Models

464 Grade K

Sound Boxes

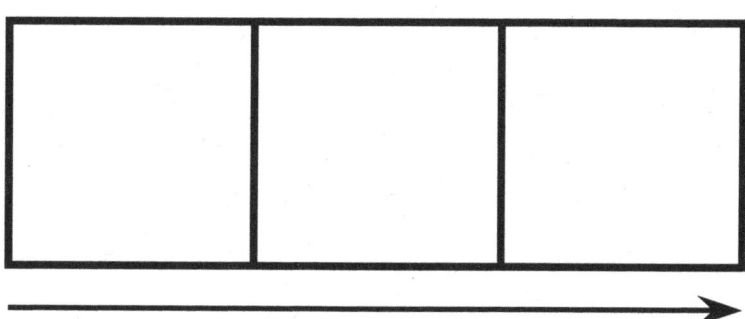

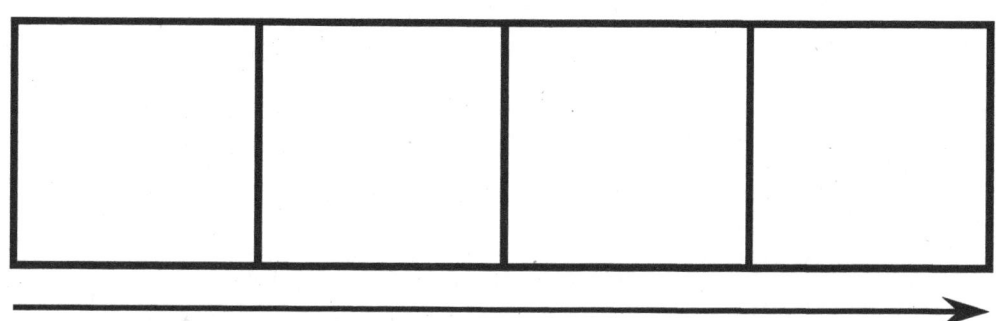

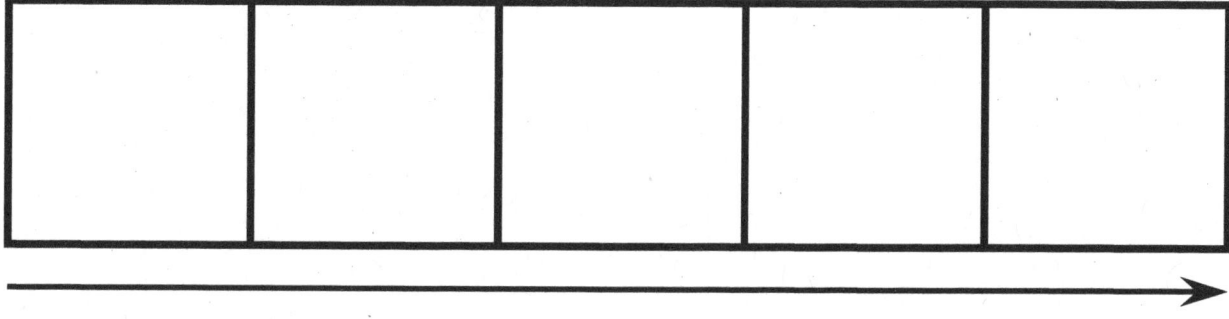

High-Frequency Word Cards

can	we	a
I	the	see

Tim **can** jump.	**I** can play.
We can see the cat.	We play in **the** sand.
Pam can use **a** ruler.	I can **see** a fish.

High-Frequency Word Cards

to	go	do
like	and	you

It is good **to** listen.	Mom and I **go** to the store.	We **do** want to go!
We **like** pizza!	I see a cat **and** a dog.	Do **you** like milk?

High-Frequency Word Cards

are	with	little
my	he	is

Ted and Ed **are** friends.	Do you like **my** hat?
I go **with** Ron to the farm.	**He** ate a red apple.
The bugs are **little**.	My bike **is** red.

High-Frequency Word Cards

was	have	of
she	for	they

Monday **was** a hot day.	Elephants **have** big ears.	I take care **of** my fish.
She can kick the ball.	This is **for** you.	**They** went to the park.

High-Frequency Word Cards

want	me	what
said	here	this

I **want** to see a lion.	The book belongs to **me**.	**What** do zebras eat?
The vet **said** Max is fine.	The bus is **here**.	I was on **this** street.

High-Frequency Word Cards

too	has	look
help	play	where

Jake can help, **too**.	I **help** to rake the leaves.
My class **has** a pet.	Mike and I **play** a game.
Look at the owl's home.	**Where** do roses grow?

High-Frequency Word Cards

good	does	
who	come	

Grade K 479

You did a **good** job.

Does this bus go north?

Who can use the paint?

Jake will **come** to my house.

Build Your Word Bank High-Frequency Word Cards

down	there	her
out	will	two

I walk **down** the hill.	Pam lives **there**.	**Her** cat is Tam.
Jim let the dog **out**.	Tim **will** help me.	I have **two** books.

Build Your Word Bank High-Frequency Word Cards

then	could	all
one	new	place

Grade K **483**

Then I went to the store.	Sam has **one** map.
I **could** do that for you.	I see her **new** hat.
Mark put **all** the cans in the box.	Nat will put the books in the right **place**.

Build Your Word Bank High-Frequency Word Cards

day	than	when
that	long	his

Grade K

What **day** of the week is it?	I wrote more **than** Nat.	I use a pen **when** I write.
Pam will use **that** map.	Dan can sing a **long** song.	Nan is **his** cat.

Build Your Word Bank High-Frequency Word Cards

many	by	now
which	them	some

Grade K 487

Bob has **many** pens.	Rob sat **by** the fan.	I can play **now**.
Which hen laid the egg?	I will ask **them** to play.	Deb will eat **some** snacks.

Build Your Word Bank High-Frequency Word Cards

from	water	people
way	how	these

Grade K

Kate drinks **from** her cup.	The **water** is hot.	Six **people** fit in the van.
Ben knows the **way** to school.	Kim knows **how** to use the lock.	Please help me move **these** boxes.

Build Your Word Bank High-Frequency Word Cards

about	or	other
work	may	each

Grade K

What **other** book do you like?	Do you like apples **or** oranges?	What is the book **about**?
We will **each** present our projects.	Jack **may** dig a big hole.	Nina will **work** hard on her homework.

Build Your Word Bank High-Frequency Word Cards

more	over	know
into	find	were

Dave can bake **more** cakes.	The gull flew **over** the lake.	I **know** you very well.
I can see **into** the cave.	Can you **find** where she is hiding?	Mike and Kate **were** late.

Build Your Word Bank High-Frequency Word Cards

write	only	first
would	part	words

Kim will **write** a play.	Dale **only** has one rose.	You are the **first** one in line.
I hoped my kite **would** fly high.	I want a **part** of the pie.	I know the **words** to the song.

Build Your Word Bank High-Frequency Word Cards

their		
sound		

I know **their** cat.

I love the **sound** of bells.

Name _____

My Concepts of Print Checklist 1

☐ Did I hold the book so it's right-side up?

☐ Did I identify the front cover of a book?

☐ Did I identify the title page of a book?

☐ Did I identify the back cover of a book?

Concepts of Print
Demonstrate the proper way to hold a book, with the front cover facing you and right-side up. Explain to children that a book has a front cover, a back cover, and a title page. Point to each one of these. Have children choose a book to read and then fill in the checklist on this page.

Name _____

My Concepts of Print Checklist 2

☐ Did I hold my book right-side up?

☐ Did I turn the pages correctly?

☐ Did I read from top to bottom?

☐ Did I read from left to right?

Concepts of Print
Model for children how to hold a book right-side up. Demonstrate also turning the pages from right to left, and reading a page from top to bottom and left to right. Tell children that when they get to the end of a line they should go to the start of the next line. Have children choose a book to read and have them demonstrate these print awareness skills. After reading, have them fill in the checklist on this page.

Name _____

My Concepts of Print Checklist 3

☐ Did I turn the pages correctly?

☐ Did I read from top to bottom?

☐ Did I read from left to right?

☐ Did I know where to read when I got to the end of the line?

Concepts of Print
Remind children to turn the pages of a book from right to left. Tell them that they need to read from left to right and from the top to the bottom of a page. Explain that when they get to the end of a line they should go to the start of the next line and continue reading. Model these concepts of print for children. Then have children choose a book to read and fill out the checklist on this page.

Name _____

My Concepts of Print Checklist 4

☐ Did I know where to read when I got to the end of a line?

☐ Can I count the words in a sentence?

☐ Did I hold the book right-side up?

☐ Did I turn the pages correctly?

Concepts of Print
Remind children that when they get to the end of a line, they need to continue reading on the next line. Point out that there is a space between each word in a sentence. Model pointing to the space between words and then how to count the number of words in a sentence. Also remind children that sentences can end with a period, a question mark, or an exclamation mark. Model these concepts of print for children. Then have children choose a book to read and fill out the checklist on this page.

Name _____

My Concepts of Print Checklist 5

☐ Did I identify the title page of a book?

☐ Did I hold the book right-side up?

☐ Did I know where to read when I got to the end of a line?

☐ Did I count the number of words in a sentence?

Concepts of Print
Remind children that a book has a front cover, a title page, and a back cover. Tell them to hold the book correctly and to turn the pages of the book from right to left. Remind them that when they get to the end of a line, they need to continue reading on the next line. Point out the difference between the letter *b* and the word *book*. Model these concepts of print for children. Then have children choose a book to read and fill out the checklist on this page.

Name _____

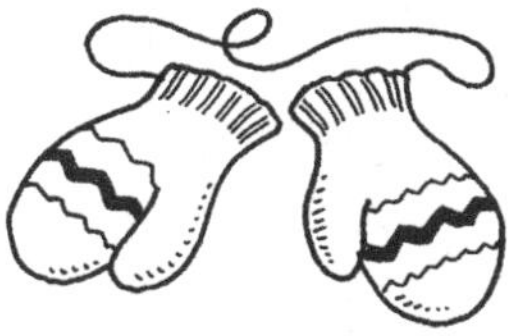

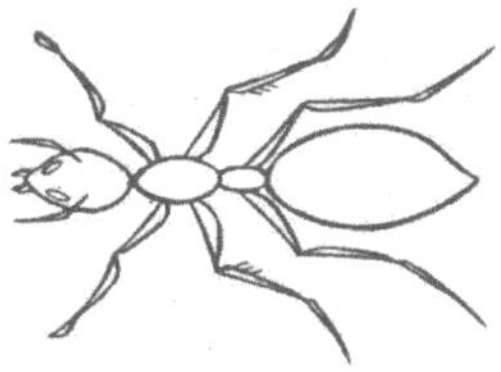

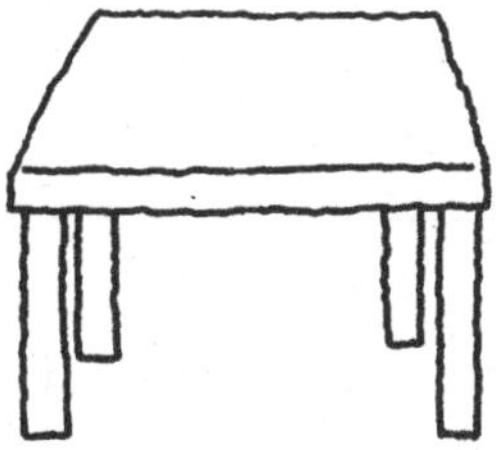

Phonics Review Game: /m/m, /a/a, /s/s, /p/p, /t/t
Say the name of each item and the letter it begins with. Turn the picture over and trace the letters. With a partner, think of other things whose names begin with each sound and letter.

Grade K • Unit 2 • Week 3 **505**

Name _____

Phonics Review Game: /m/m, /a/a, /s/s, /p/p, /t/t
Trace the letters. Say each letter and its sound. Then name a word that begins with the letter.

Name _____

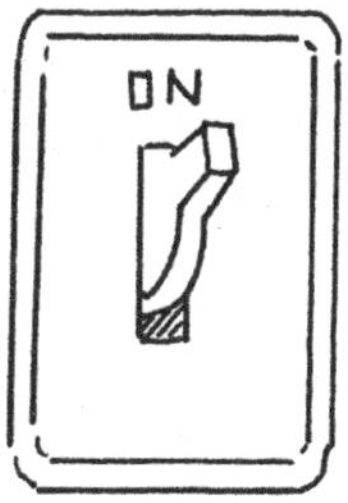

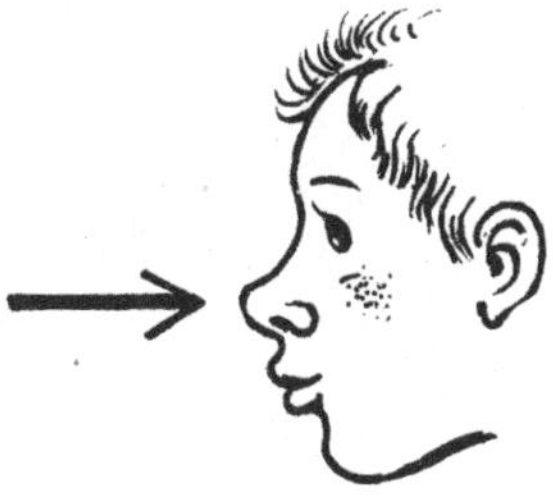

Phonics Review Game: /i/i, /n/n, /k/c, /o/o, /d/d
Say the name of each item and the letter it begins with. Then cut out each picture.

Grade K • Unit 4 • Week 3

Name _____

Phonics Review Game: /i/i, /n/n, /k/c, /o/o, /d/d
Place the picture cards face-down onto a desk or table. Flip two cards over and say the names of the pictures. Have children say the letter that stands for each beginning sound. If the pictures begin with the same letter, you have made a match. Continue playing until all cards have been matched.

Name _____

Phonics Review Game: /h/h, /e/e, /f/f, /r/r, /b/b, /l/l
Place a marker on "Start." Move your marker from square to square. When you land on a picture, say the name of the picture and the letter it begins with. If you land on a letter, say a word that begins with that letter. You may also wish to distribute cards with the numbers 1, 2, and 3 for children to use to move however many spaces the card says. When you reach "End," play again and think of new words.

Name _____

b   ck

Phonics Review Game: /b/b, /k/ck
Say the name of each picture. Draw lines to connect the pictures to the letters they end with. Work with a partner to think of other words that end with each of these sounds. Then use the words in sentences.

Name _____

Phonics Review Game: /u/u, /g/g, /w/w, /v/v, /j/j, /kw/qu, /y/y, /z/z
Place a marker on "Start." Move your marker from square to square. When you land on a picture, say the name of the picture and the letter it begins with. If you land on a letter, say a word that begins with that letter. You may also wish to distribute 3 cards with a number on each one. When you reach "End," play again and think of new words.

Grade K • Unit 8 • Week 3   **511**

 Name _____

   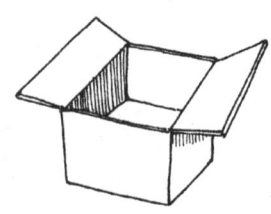

g   x

Phonics Review Game: /g/g, /ks/x
Say the name of each picture. Draw lines to connect the pictures to the letters they end with. Encourage pairs of children to think of other words that end with these sounds. Tell them to work with a partner and use the words in sentences.

Name _____

Phonics Review Game: /ā/a_e, /ī/i_e, /ō/o_e, /ū/u_e, /ē/e, ee
Cut on the dotted lines. Fold on the solid lines and tape together to make a cube.

Name _____

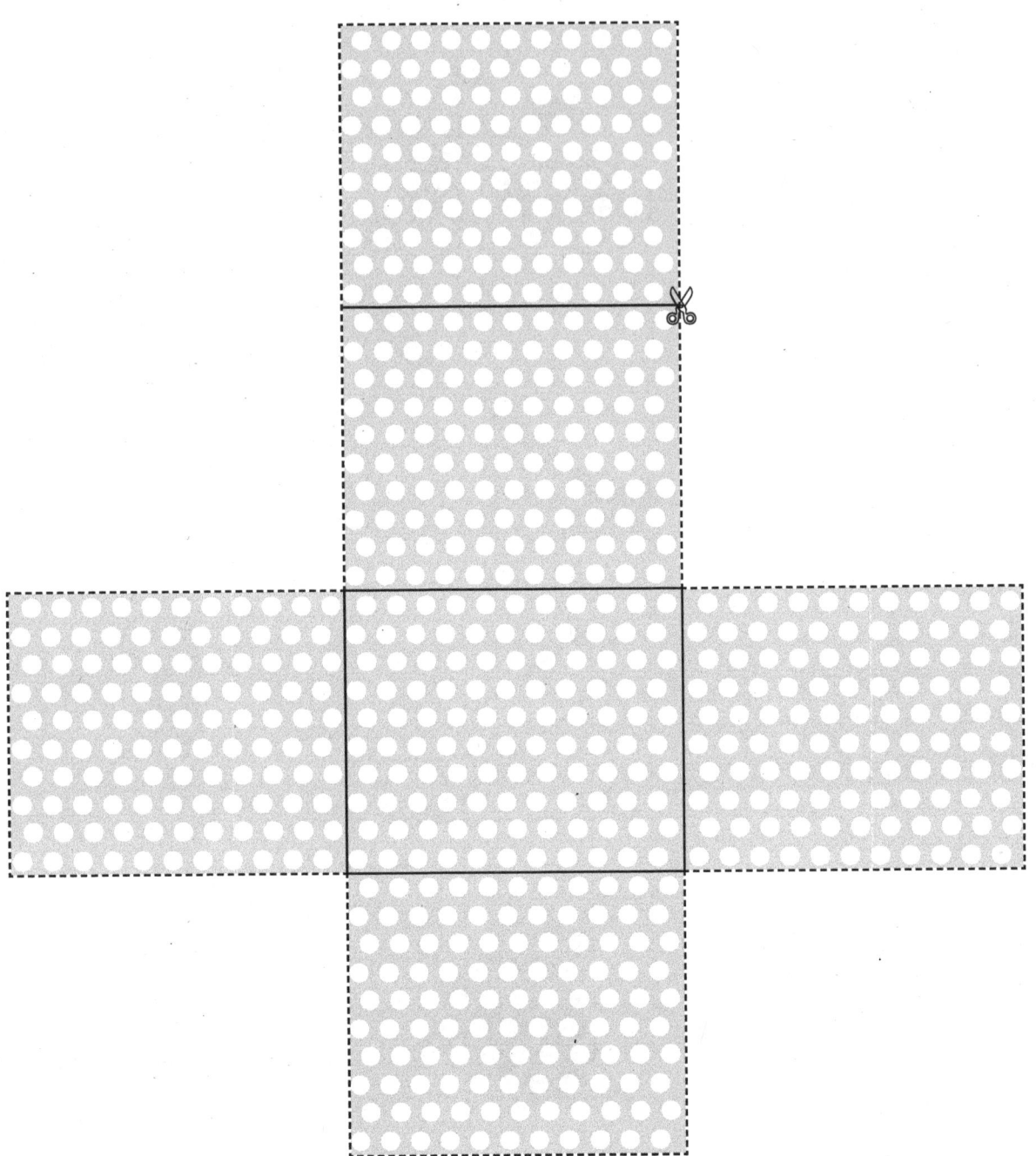

Phonics Review Game: /ā/a_e, /ī/i_e, /ō/o_e, /ū/u_e, /ē/e, ee
Toss the cube with a partner. Say the name of the picture that faces up. Say the long vowel sound you hear in the word. Then say another word that has that long vowel sound.

My Strategies and Tools

Listen Carefully

Listen with your WHOLE BODY!

- eyes watching
- brain thinking
- mouth quiet
- ears listening
- heart caring
- body facing the speaker
- hands still
- feet still

Ask Questions

Asking questions can help you understand what you read.

Before

Ask about

- the title, art, or photos.
- what you will find out.
- what you want to understand.

During

Ask about

- ideas you do not understand.
- words you do not know.
- the characters in a story.
- an event from a text.

After

Ask about

- something you still want to understand.
- more information you want to know.

Important Details

Key details are the most important details.
Find key details in the text, pictures, or photos.

Details

Spot is Jim's best friend.
Jim and Spot like to run.
Jim and Spot like to jump.
They have fun together.

Key Details

Spot is Jim's best friend.
They have fun together.

Read a text with a partner.
Talk about the details.
Identify the important details.

Retell a Text

When you retell a text, you tell the important details.

1. Look at the pictures on each page.
2. Tell your partner the important details in order.
3. Take turns with your partner.

Respond to a Text

Share what you learn about a text. Use text evidence in your response. Make a connection to the text. Use new words you learned.

Talk About It

- Talk to a partner.
- Discuss the topic. Talk about what the text is about.
- Tell how you connected to the text.

Write About It

- Write complete sentences.
- Read your writing.

Draw a Picture

- Write labels.
- Talk about your picture.

Make a Connection

Make a connection to what you read. Share your connection with a partner.

> This connects to a time when I ...

> This connects to another book I read because ...

> This connects to my world because ...

Research Plan

Follow the steps.

Step 1
Choose a topic.
- What do you want to find out about?

Step 2
Write your questions.
- What do you want to learn?

Step 3
Decide where to find the answers.
- Talk to an expert or read a text.
- Find the information you need.

Step 4
Write what you learn.
- Draw pictures.
- Write the answers to your questions.

Step 5
Choose how to present your work.

Write about it!   Create a model.

Do a demonstration.

Share what you learned!

Choose a Book

How to choose a book:
- Pick a book. Open it to any page.
- Read all the words on the page.
- Put one finger up for each word you can't figure out.

Five Finger Rule

	0 – 1 Fingers	This book will be easy for you. Make sure you don't choose too many books that are too easy for you.
	2 – 3 Fingers	This is a great choice!
	4 Fingers	Give this book a try.
	5 Fingers	This is a challenging book. You might want to make another choice.

Now spend time reading. Try to read a little longer each time.

Who Is Telling the Story?

Listen to the story. Talk about who is telling the story. Is it a character who tells the story or a narrator who tells the story?

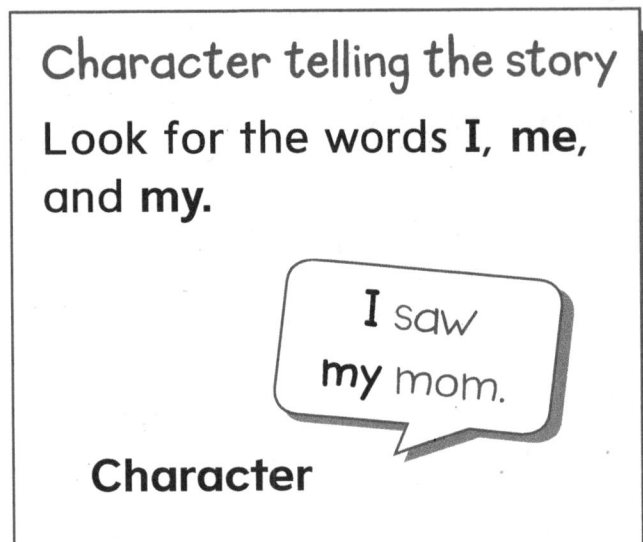

Character telling the story

Look for the words **I**, **me**, and **my**.

I saw my mom.

Character

Narrator telling the story

Look for the words **he**, **she**, **they**, and **characters' names**.

They saw a bird.

Narrator

Combine Information

Each page of a text gives you information. The information on every page is connected. Sometimes new information can change what you understand about a text.

= What I Learned

- Read a page.
  Tell a partner what you learned.

- Read another page.
  Tell a partner what you learned.
  Did your understanding of the text change?

- Tell how the information is connected.
  Take turns with your partner.

Make Inferences

Sometimes an author does not tell you some information.

- Think about clues in the text or pictures.
- Think about what you already know.
- Put the clues and what you know together.
- Make an inference.

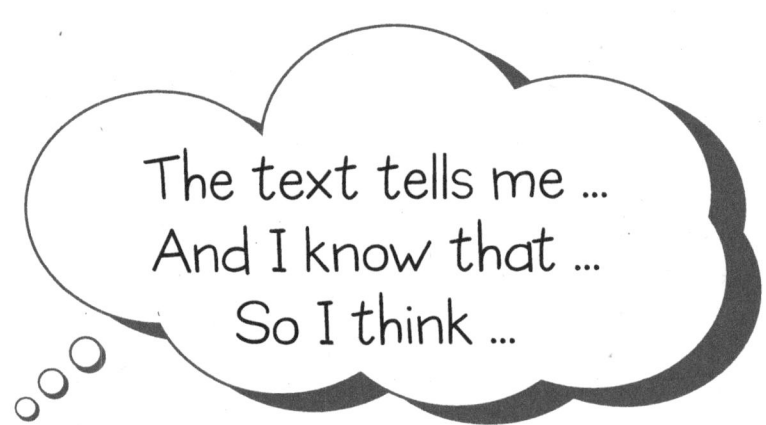

The text tells me ...
And I know that ...
So I think ...

Make a Prediction

A prediction is a guess about what will happen next. To make a prediction, you can use information from the text.

> Text Features
>
> Look at the photos and illustrations.
> Look at the captions.
> What information will you learn?

> Text Structure
>
> Talk about how the text is organized.
> What happened first?
> What may happen next?

Check Your Prediction

Check to see if your predictions are correct. If they are not correct, you can always change them.

Text Features

Look at the photos and illustrations.

Look at the captions.

What information did you learn?

Text Structure

Think about how the text is organized.

What happened?

Name _____

My Notes

Name _____

My Notes

Name _____

My Notes

Name _____

My Notes

Name _____

My Notes

Name _____

My Notes

Credits

Wonders Practice Book Grade K Volume 1 Student Edition: *Chapter from Wonders Practice Book Grade K Volume 1 Student Edition, 2020* 1